life *interrupted*

Spalding Gray

life *interrupted*
THE UNFINISHED MONOLOGUE

CROWN PUBLISHERS
NEW YORK

Photographs on pages 50 and 116 courtesy of Noah
Greenberg; photograph on page 110 courtesy of Jupiter
Images Corporation.

Published in the United States by Crown Publishers, an
imprint of the Crown Publishing Group, a division of
Random House, Inc., New York.
www.crownpublishing.com

Crown is a trademark and the Crown colophon is a
registered trademark of Random House, Inc.

Library of Congress Cataloging-in-Publication Data
Gray, Spalding, 1941–2004
  Life interrupted : the unfinished monologue /
    Spalding Gray.—1st ed.
  Includes bibliographical references and index.
  1. Gray, Spalding, 1941–2004.   2. Performance
artists—United States—Biography.   3. Traffic accident
victims—United States—Biography.   4. Depression,
Mental—Patients—United States—Biography.
  I. Title.
  PS3557.R333L54 2005
  812'.54—dc22   2005001592

ISBN 1-4000-4861-3

Printed in the United States of America

DESIGN BY ELINA D. NUDELMAN

10 9 8 7 6 5 4 3 2 1

First Edition

FOR MARISSA, FORREST, AND THEO
AND OTHER SURVIVORS OF SUICIDE

acknowledgments

Kathleen Russo would like to thank the following people for making this book possible:

Suzanne Gluck for always believing in Spalding and his work.

Annik LaFarge for her commitment to and enthusiasm for this project, her assistant, Mario Rojas, and the entire staff at Crown.

Stokes Howell for listening to every word.

Mark Russell and the staff at P.S. 122 for presenting Spalding and helping him develop the piece.

Jamie Askin, Katherine Atkinson, Josh Blum and the staff of Washington Square Arts/Films, Nancy Campbell, George Coates, Gracie Coates,

Joe and Joan Cullman, Leon Falk, William Farley, John Fine, Ted Fine, Norman Frisch, Alison Granucci, Jim and Muniera Griffiths, Tamara Hill, Coleman Hough, Janet Jacobs, Jennifer Lambert, Colleen Larkin, Julie Nives, Doug Pepper, Pallas Pidgeon, Rev. Billy, Susan Roxbury, Richard Shechner, Liam Scott and family, Mary Shimkin, Paul Spencer, Philip Stanton, Barney Strauss, Marlene Swartz, Marcelle Tosi, and all the people who supported the evolution of *Life Interrupted*.

Howie Michaels and Francine Prose.

Bernard Gersten and the Lincoln Center staff.

Patrick Murphy, Patricia Murphy, and all the nurses who worked with Spalding in Ireland.

Claire Callahan and all the warm people from Ireland who opened their homes to us.

Tara Newman and Caroline Beegan for being there after the accident.

ACKNOWLEDGMENTS

John Perry Barlow, Lorraine and Alex Cooper, Terry Hyland, Donald Lipski, the Harringtons, and everyone who helped us in the States after the accident.

To Deirdre Guest, Harbor Music, Jennifer Houser, Kevin Inkawitch, Ken Kinna, Janet O'Brien, Dale Scott, the Stelle family, Sara Vass, Cati Von Milders, the Whaling Church staff, the Whelen family, Rez and Lucy Williams, the Wooster Group, and everyone who helped with both memorials.

Teresa and Cienna Quinn for always being there when we need them.

To Robby Stein, for his ongoing support and love and for being the best godfather to the children.

To Spalding's best friend, Ken Kobland. For almost forty years, Spalding cherished your conversations and companionship. Thank you for your unconditional love.

ACKNOWLEDGMENTS

Spalding's brothers, Rocky and Chan, and their families, Mom, Dad, Karen, Duke, Peter, Maureen, Paul, Marissa, Forrest, Theo, and the rest of the Russo/Gray clan for their love and support.

Dave O for his compassion and love.

Most of all, to Spalding—may his stories go on forever . . .

contents

CONTENTS

CONTENTS

life interrupted

foreword

By Francine Prose

Years ago, I heard a novelist say that his most cherished fantasy was to sit at a small wooden desk in the middle of Yankee Stadium. On the desk he would have his typewriter, the tall black old-fashioned Royal to which he had a superstitious attachment, and which turned writing into a form of fairly strenuous physical exercise. He'd write a sentence; the crowd would watch. Another sentence, and he could sense the fans moving toward the edge of their seats. And then at last he would write a particularly brilliant and beautiful sentence, and the stadium would erupt in a mad frenzy of applause, cheers, and whistles.

As far as I know, my novelist friend never

got his wish. But it's often occurred to me that what he imagined was an exaggerated but essentially accurate description of Spalding's working method.

Spalding wrote at a small wooden desk in front of an audience; the only thing missing was the typewriter. He constructed his monologues by telling and retelling his stories, and he revised them in public, from performance to performance. Stories would be added and dropped, shortened and lengthened, rearranged, emphasized and de-emphasized as, like most artists, he discovered what he was trying to do only in the process of trying to do it. In these early stages of a work, he was always—as he almost always was—multitasking. He seemed somehow capable of talking and listening at the same time. Even as he was narrating anecdotes and episodes from his own life, he managed to be exquisitely attentive to how the audience was responding and to what he was getting back from the crowd. What stories were working, what was and wasn't making people laugh, the momentary lapses in attention and interest that a performer can feel opening up like black holes into which the entire evening can disappear.

Much of this would have been clear to fans who saw his work in various stages of completion. An early draft of *Swimming to Cambodia*—which might well be Spalding's masterpiece—was four hours long, and was performed over two successive evenings. The final version, and the one that appeared in the film, was half that length—a pared-down, concentrated, and improved version, though there were elements in the longer draft that I loved, and remembered, and missed.

In any case, what Spalding's friends knew was that, for him, the process of composing a monologue began long before he ever walked out on stage and sat behind his little wooden desk and took a sip from his glass of water. It began over dinner, or on the telephone, or during a chance encounter on the street, when—in response to a question about where he'd been or what he'd been doing—he'd pause, and then, completely deadpan, launch into the hilarious or horrifying account of all the bizarre things that had happened to him since the last time we'd seen him.

In his famous essay "The Storyteller," the critic Walter Benjamin quotes a German proverb: "When someone goes on a trip, he has something to tell about." And to those of us who knew and loved Spalding, it always seemed as if he were just going on, or returning from, a trip, even when the journey had taken him no farther than a walk through the neighborhood he so loved, downtown Manhattan.

He adored the city, and adapted to the ways in which it changed even as he fiercely held on to an image of how the city used to be in the rougher and more bohemian 1970s, when he had arrived in Manhattan; at that time, SoHo was still an artists' community, a small village of painters and poets and actors, and had not yet turned into an upmarket mall. He felt a great tenderness for New York, and for the great variety and vitality of its residents. And his *Dear New York City* is an expression of that tenderness, a love letter to the city at its most wounded and vulnerable moment, to that "island off the coast of America where human nature was king and everyone exuded character and had big attitude."

All Spalding had to do was walk out his front door and odd people gravitated to him, strange things happened, things that would not have happened to anyone else. And what his accounts of his childhood—including the stories in *Sex and Death to the Age 14*—suggest is that he was somehow born that way, born with the capacity to see and hear and experience a little more, a little more deeply and widely, than most everyone else.

Part of what made him such a magnet for the unusual, such a likely mark for the demented ravings of every sort of obsessive, crank, extremist, and lunatic was his absolute openness, his commitment to considering every possibility, to refrain from judging, from jumping to form the sorts of quick, facile, conventional opinions that most people—well, most *reasonable* people—might reasonably entertain.

Spalding liked to think of himself as a Buddhist. Once, I interviewed him for *Tricycle,* the Buddhist magazine; I imagine that anyone who actually knew anything about Buddhism would probably have quickly concluded that both of us were making it up as we went along, but that didn't make our conversation any less searching or heartfelt. I think that part of what Buddhism meant to Spalding involved a series of brief maxims having to do with consciousness and conduct. Axioms like: First thought, best thought. No judgment. That sort of thing. And strangers opened up to him, told him things they would not normally have told a stranger because they intuited—and people have an unusual awareness, almost a sixth sense for this sort of thing—that he would listen and not judge them. He listened, he really listened, in a way that few people ever manage to do, and his reward was that people told him stories that he could recycle, and make part of his own story, his art.

That was partly why *Interviewing the Audience* was one of the works I loved most, and perhaps the one I saw most often, because it was always different, and always fascinating. Before each performance, Spalding would circulate among the people waiting to see the show, asking for volunteers to join him on stage and participate in what had to have been the most gentle, low-key, reflective, and odd interview process imaginable. He had an uncanny eye for choosing people who had something exceptional and even startling to report, and he could (correctly, it seemed to me) discover the zeitgeist of an entire city or region of the country from the kinds of stories its citizens told, and their willingness to tell them. Meanwhile, for the audience, the experience of watching people open up and express what was in their hearts and minds always felt a little like playing with one of those astonishing children's toys: those little sponges you put in water and watch as they swell into a flower or a tiny dinosaur.

Spalding had an enormous hunger for, and

curiosity about, experience of every sort. He was game; he would try anything to see what it felt like and how it worked. He seemed to lack the sort of self-consciousness that keeps most people from doing things they fear might prove embarrassing or compromise their dignity. There was almost no invitation that he would turn down, and if he did, he would be consumed with regret about what marvelous things would have happened had he only been braver, and accepted. He always longed to be in at least two places at once, to live as many concurrent lives as possible, and *Swimming to Cambodia* is partly about that desire. Even when his health—his life—was at stake he remained open to the siren song of possibility. When he developed a problem with his vision, he experimented with therapies that most of us wouldn't even consider, and *Gray's Anatomy* records his unlikely and hilarious pilgrim's progress from sweat lodge to charlatan to the marginally more trust-inspiring frontiers of traditional medicine.

The running joke of nearly every monologue is the way in which everything that happens to him seems to reflect—in a humorous and slightly creepy way that cannot be explained even by the laws of chance—and refer to everything else that has been happening to him; everything is a reminder of his deepest worries, fears, and obsessions. It's something that many of us have discovered: Experience seems to follow a pattern, and incidents clump together in ways that intensify and confirm our (often darkest) premonitions and preoccupations. Fate and coincidence conspire to keep us in a fun house lined with mirrors glittering with images drawn up from the deep well of our own psyche.

Spalding found in life, as so many artists do, what he was looking for—what he needed—

for his work. It wasn't anything half so simple as life imitating art. It was far more mysterious, something more like art guiding life, making things happen according to the needs of art. When he had finished *Morning, Noon and Night*, his hymn to happiness and domestic contentment, to the joy he had finally found in being with his Kathie, Marissa, Forrest, and Theo, he worried that he would no longer be able to write any more monologues. He was afraid that the elements he had needed—anxiety, conflict, doubt, trouble—for his work were no longer present in his life. As he says in *Life Interrupted*, "My life is without crisis and usually they're based on crisis. . . . Things are going smoothly." When he performed the piece, he knocked on wood. He knew that to say something like that was to tempt fate. And it proved to be all the temptation, all the provocation, fate needed. Because no sooner did he say that than he had the catastrophic accident that would provide the "material" for a new monologue, the one that would be his last.

I remember it very clearly. It was the summer of 2001. A bright June Sunday morning. We were in our home in upstate New York, on the farm where our friendship with Spalding began, where he lived with Howie and me and our two sons, in our little guesthouse, for two summers in the early 1980s. Spalding had first driven up on a cold winter afternoon in 1982 because he was looking for a cottage to rent in the country. Often, during those months, we would see him walking around the property and mumbling into the tape recorder on which he experimented with practice drafts of the narratives that would go into his monologues. And by the end of that summer, we had become close friends—as it would turn out—for life.

On that summer morning, in 2001, I checked my e-mail, and found a message from a mutual friend, April Gornik, saying that Spalding and Kathie had been involved in a serious auto accident in Ireland. Spalding was gravely injured; he was in the hospital. I immediately called another friend, Robby Stein, who had the phone number of Spalding's hospital room in Ireland. I phoned, and Spalding answered.

There is a very particular, very specific kind of relief we feel when we have been deeply worried about someone we love, and then we see the person, or hear the person's voice, and realize that the person is still alive and with us, still in the world. I realized that something awful had happened, but when I heard Spalding's voice—familiar, laconic, with that unmistakable New England accent he never lost—what I felt was joy, pure joy. I'd been in terror, and the terror instantly melted away.

I remember it very clearly. I was sitting outside, on the patio, on the vintage pink couch that is in fact something like a cross between a sofa and a porch swing. I rocked myself, for comfort, as I talked to Spalding, and then I no longer needed the comfort of rocking, because comfort was streaming through the phone line, across the ocean, from a hospital room in Ireland to the sunny patio in upstate New York.

It was instantly obvious that whatever had happened to Spalding hadn't in the least affected his sense of humor. He was, it seemed, in good spirits, despite everything. He told me about the collision with the veterinarian rushing to make a house call, and about the vials of medicine lying all over the road, and a series of hilarious horror stories, one after another, about the dirtiness of the hospital and the oddities of the staff and of his fellow patients. It felt just as it always had, listening to the stories coming together, being the guinea-pig audience, present at the inception of something just starting to take shape. I asked him if he was writing all of this down. He said he was taking notes. And then we had a long conversation about how ironic and amazing it was: how he'd been worried that he would never find another subject for a monologue, afraid that he was too happy, too content to go on writing. And now this had happened to him, providing him with subject matter, with new stories he could turn into art. Yes, he said, he knew. How amazing. How ironic. Before we hung up, he told me a few more stories about his stay in Ireland—the dark premonitions he'd had before the crash— and again it felt just as it always had when Spalding was telling stories that, I knew, would reappear in his monologues, changed and edited and transformed into art.

We said our good-byes. I told him to get

better quickly. I said we'd come visit as soon as he got back to New York.

It was the last normal, happy conversation we ever had.

A series of operations followed the accident. One on his hip, another on his brain. Spalding was clearly weak, shaken, disturbed about the prospects for a full recovery. And yet throughout much of his final illness, even when his depression became so severe that he was barely able to hold a simple conversation, he was, miraculously, able to perform, and in fact he seemed better when he was touring, on stage, working.

Life Interrupted began as a sort of introduction to the performances he gave of *Interviewing the Audience* at festivals in Seattle and Chicago in the late summer of 2001. When *Swimming to Cambodia* was revived at the Performing Garage, where Spalding's career as a monologuist had begun, the new material again functioned as a prologue to the older piece. He tried it out everywhere he toured in 2002, and then at P.S. 122, where he performed on Sunday and Monday nights from mid-October 2003 until December 16, not long before his death. He did the new monologue in progress and read *The Anniversary*, which seemed like a sort of companion piece because it shared some of the same themes and concerns.

From the very beginning, the tone of *Life Interrupted* is laid-back, relaxed, offhand, yet somehow confident and authoritative; that is to say, pure Spalding. "Whimsical" is the word he used to describe Ireland, but it could just as easily refer to himself. And yet right from the very beginning, or almost the very beginning, there's that disturbing note that seems just as characteristic, just as typical.

If there was one thing Spalding knew about, and talked about, and captured perhaps better than anyone else in contemporary literature or theater, it was that moment in which you're at peace, at rest, or even enjoying yourself, having fun . . . and suddenly there's that disturbing, bass-note thrum, that chill as if someone's opened a door and let a cold draft into the room, that dark thread you can follow if you want (and Spalding always wanted to) all the way to the brick wall, to the fact of your own mortality. It happens often in literature as well as life, in stories that range from Poe's "The Masque of the Red Death" to Joyce's "The Dead." There's a knock on the door, or no knock at all, or someone makes an ill-advised remark, and suddenly Death is present, uninvited, at the party.

One of the things about Spalding that gave his work its freshness, its unique combination of innocence and sophistication was what you might call his chronic Peter Panism: his resolute, even stubborn refusal to let himself be deadened and consoled and bought in those ways that are commonly referred to as "growing up." Perhaps that was part of the reason why he was always, as they say, good with children. The first summer he came to live with us, I was pregnant with our younger son. It was not the easiest summer for our older son, Bruno, who was then four. For though we tried to prepare him for his brother's birth, to make him realize that our love for him would not be diminished by the addition of a new family member, he sensed that great changes were on the way, changes that would not necessarily be to his liking.

That summer, Bruno and Spalding developed a friendship based, like so much in Spalding's life, on ritual. You might say it was the early-morning equivalent of Spalding's sacred early-evening cocktail hour. I don't know if Spalding actually liked Cheerios. But he kept them on hand, and every morning, Bruno would walk across the yard and have breakfast— Cheerios with milk and banana—with Spalding. I don't think they talked much; Spalding treated children with the same reserved, almost solemn politeness with which he treated adults, and listened in the same way he listened to grown-ups. Kids loved it, and that summer, Bruno's friendship with Spalding was one of the things that helped him remain hopeful, calm, and secure. Spalding's affinity for children was so profound and so obvious that though he claimed that he just wanted to be "a sweet mellow uncle figure for someone else's kids," we always thought he should have a family of his own, and so the passion with which he fell in love with his own children came as less of a shock to us than it seemed to be for him.

He preserved, and insisted on preserving, a child's sense of wonder—and what came along with it was a child's astonished, outraged response to the cruelty, the unfairness, the sheer awfulness of death. In several of the monologues he described being a small boy and listening to the rhythmic conversation, almost a sort of lullaby, with which his mother (whose madness and suicide had such a powerful effect on him and played such an essential role in so much of his work) put his brother to sleep. "I just lay there listening and staring up at the only light in the room, the fluorescent decals of the moon and stars on the ceiling. I lay there and Rocky started in and said, 'Mom, when I die, will it be forever?' And Mom answered him with this beautiful calm tone of voice so simple and slow. She just said, 'Yes, dear.' Then Rocky said it again and again, and each time he asked her he would add another 'forever,' and each time Mom would give this steady slow affirmative response." Near the end of *Morning, Noon and Night* there is a long and heartbreakingly beautiful meditation, one I still cannot read without tears, inspired by the question of how to explain the fact of death to the metaphysically minded Forrest and eventually to baby Theo:

> So, what do I tell my boys when they come to me with their questions on death? Forrest already had. He started asking me about death before he was four and I told him that everyone who is born must one day die. Then I told him that the funny thing about that . . . or odd thing, because death is rarely funny, is that everyone knows they're going to die but no one really believes it.

This is a big and important fact, I told him.
This is, in fact, what I consider the reality of the
world. He seemed to take this in. I don't know what
Forrest did with it, but he listened and he took it in.

And apparently, Forrest did. Because *Life Interrupted* begins, more or less, where *Morning, Noon and Night* left off. In the middle of Spalding's sixtieth birthday party, Forrest asks his father if he remembers how much fun birthdays used to be before he found out that he was going to die.

Indeed, even before Spalding leaves for Ireland, death is everywhere. Their host, whose manor they will be staying in, has died two weeks before. The manor itself recalls the hotel in Kubrick's *The Shining*. They're in the town of Mort, not far from a monastery where Spalding sees the grave diggers taking a break from their labors. The radio station features local obituaries; at the end of a hike Spalding takes, a sick calf appears, like a macabre premonition. And then comes the crash, the noise and violence, the blood, the ambulance, the hospital.

Even in the midst of it, Spalding is still monitoring, observing, paying attention to the world and to the people around him. Even in the small country hospital, he continues to be a magnet for the unusual, the eccentric, and the extreme; the person bringing tea and toast to the ward is not your standard-issue nurse or hospital volunteer but, rather, a cross-dresser with long green fingernails. And in the depth of his own pain and worry and chaos, he's hearing other people's stories, listening to his roommate's account of how he lost a leg in a train accident.

In these early pages, all the old themes begin to resurface, and it's impossible not to think about how, in time, Spalding would have been able to orchestrate them, to raise and lower the volume and the pitch of each of these subsidiary melodies. The body—its needs and desires, its limits and its imperatives—was always a subject to which Spalding returned, and to which the events of his life kept bringing him back. Physicality was immensely important to him; the monologues are filled with sheer activity—skiing, swimming, dancing, bike riding—and, as Spalding mentions his reluctance to watch Wimbledon on TV ("What do I want to watch a bunch of people playing tennis for when I can't play it anymore? It's hard for me to watch those beautiful bodies moving so fast"), *Life Interrupted* begins to confront the physical problems that so heavily contributed to the overwhelming sense of grief and loss that ended Spalding's life. When a friend suggests that Spalding consider going out to Santa Fe to see a healer whose regimen involves burying all one's money and surviving on Campbell's celery soup, we hear echoes of *Gray's Anatomy*, and perhaps hints of the direction in which the monologue might have gone in the future—if there had been a future.

As Spalding became more well known, he compensated for his inability to be an invisible, unnoticed observer with a new sort of attentiveness: an ironic awareness of his own recognition factor, who recognized him and who didn't, what fans and strangers thought of him and his work. So, here, he and the house staff discuss his movie roles, and his mention on *The Simpsons* is at once a bright spot and a painful contrast to the darker reality of his situation. In fact, it's all here—politics (the quick reference to George Bush and the litigiousness of American society), religion (the nonpracticing Catholic nurse), the unanswerable interrogations and courage of one's children. Coincidence—

fate's calling card, its sly trick—is very much in evidence; an unlikely percentage of the people Spalding encounters turn out to be named Murphy. And, as always, there is the subject of death: the death of Andy Warhol, of Spalding's neighbor Carlos, of Thumper, the pet rabbit. But ultimately—in its present form, and again you can't help imagining how much deeper and fuller, richer and more layered it would have been in its final version—the monologue ends with a nod to survival, and to the ways to survive. Wear your seat belt. Get a credit card that will pay for your speedy exit from a place of danger to a place of what—at least at first— seems like relative safety.

If you had to reduce all of Spalding's work to its essence, its core, if you wanted to locate the subject to which, no matter what else he talked about, he kept returning, I suppose you could say that his work was a profoundly metaphysical inquiry into how we manage to live despite the knowledge that we are someday going to die. How are we to love the world and the people we care about most even when we know that someday we will lose it all and our loved ones will have to continue without us?

The Anniversary is a fitting companion piece to *Life Interrupted,* partly because it does consider so many of the same questions, but also because the fragment we have here contains something as close to pure affirmation as anything we find in Spalding's work.

Like *Life Interrupted,* it begins with one of those moments—well, several of those moments—when, in the midst of ordinary life, you suddenly watch a glint of the light that seems to be shining directly off the Grim Reaper's scythe. The piece begins with an echo of Elizabeth's Gray's eerie verbal lullaby, with the early-

morning anxiety about disappearing "forever
and ever, and ever, and forever." But if, as Spalding said, there was nothing funny about death,
he always managed to find *something* comical
about it. And here it's Theo's desire to play the
Mummy, to transform his death-obsessed father into a pretend corpse whose brain is about
to be devoured by flesh-eating beetles.

The Anniversary charts a day, a typical day—
that is to say, a day during which the forces of
damage and disaster are locked in their usual
daily battle with the life force, with the power
of pleasure and joy. There are reasons for grief
and suffering everywhere: in the terrible fate
that has befallen Spalding's friend Freya, who,
after a series of strokes, hovers in a "horrific
bardo state. Somewhere in between living and
dying . . . some limbo state where time does
not exist." And in the sorrow of the relatives
who camp out by the hospital bedside of Spald-

ing's neighbor Carlos, who lies ill and probably dying of pneumonia. And yet the life force keeps insisting on itself. Though the doctors have given her husband a one percent chance of survival, Carlos's wife, Marie, remains certain that he is going to pull through. As they leave the hospital, Spalding is moved to pray for what only a miracle will accomplish: "I visualized a warm ball of energy at the base of my spine. It looked like a little sun. Then I let it rise up my spine and burst out the top of my head. It burst out like a volcano of multicolored confetti, and it sprayed up and out and settled on Carlos like a colorful electric snow."

And now *The Anniversary* moves into what (in its present form) is its joyous final section: the merry-go-round ride he takes with Theo.

We were the only ones on the merry-go-round and it was going very fast. Theo was on an outside horse, and I on the horse just in from him. I looked over at Theo going up and down to the music and I saw that he was very, very happy. He was purely, utterly, very happy. There was no room for anything else but the happiness that filled him.

I don't remember who did it first, but . . . no, it was me . . . or was it I? Anyway, I let out with a yell that was sort of half performed and half spontaneously real. In other words, I was quite aware of it coming out of me and how it sounded. And I do know that it was my yell that triggered Theo, and he just lifted his head back and let out with this yelping, joyful cry. It was like out of a movie, only better. His cry just grabbed the whole day by the feet, by the short hairs, and gathered it up. It was pure celebration. It was unadulterated happiness.

Every life is as valuable and important as every other life, just as every absence leaves a unique hole in the fabric of the world that cannot be mended or filled. And yet it's a simple fact that there are people we miss more than others, whose absence grieves us more than we would have thought possible. And Spalding is one of those.

As I write this, it's been almost a year since his death. What I missed at the beginning, I realize now, had to do with the past, with the friendship we'd shared, and which had come to an untimely and tragic end. But now I have come to understand that what I mourn most has to do with the present and the future, with learning to live in the world without Spalding in it. There was no one like Spalding. No one's mind, no one's sensibility functioned in quite the same way: He was always surprising, always interesting, always seeing things in ways that would never have occurred to anyone else. Often I find myself wanting to hear what he would say about something: a film, a play, an item I read in the newspaper. And now that our country has fallen on such difficult and frightening times, it seems to me that we need him more than ever. What all of us wouldn't give to hear that calm, reflective, thoughtful voice commenting on the precipice on which our nation seems to be standing.

If there is a consolation, it's what he left behind: the children whom he so loved and, of course, his work. Reading the unfinished pieces in this volume, reading back through his published monologues, watching the films of his stage performances, we hear his voice again and feel the happiness we felt when he sat on stage behind his wooden desk, took a sip from his water glass, transformed the raw material of his life into art, and the crowd applauded each brilliant, beautiful sentence.

LIFE INTERRUPTED

I didn't think there'd be another monologue, and I'm still not sure if there is. I had settled down into domesticity and a quiet life out in Sag Harbor and didn't want to continue making family soap opera. Or at least I thought I didn't.

When I turned sixty there was no big celebration, just a family gathering. I said I didn't want anything. NPR did announce it on *Morning Edition,* I was happy to hear. Garrison Keillor did not, on his birthday show. We're not exactly on the best of terms. I reviewed a book of his called *Leaving Home* in the *New York Times,* and I opened with my girlfriend at the time saying that if I played that show *Prairie Home Companion* again she'd throw the radio out the window.

There was no party, just a birthday dinner at home, and I remember Forrest, my eight-year-old, saying, "Hey, Dad, remember how much fun it was having a birthday before you found out that you were going to die?"

Then there was a surprise. About two weeks after that, Kathie, my wife, gave me a present of a trip to Ireland for the whole family. Kathie's always coming up with these crazy trips. I remember she took us to the Ice Hotel up in Quebec City where you pay three hundred dollars a night to sleep on a block of ice. So Ireland was cushy. It was a rainy version of the Ice Hotel, I suppose. A little more whimsical, and rainy, and not frozen. I'd been six times before and wanted to go back. It made me laugh in a way that the United States doesn't. We had rainy times but good times. In spite of the rain it was a jolly place. I can remember Kathie and me riding bikes in the rain for hours and then coming upon this Irishman leaning against his bicycle with a golf hat on or whatever they wear, and he said, "How are you doing?" I said, "It's just awful weather, it's just awful," and he said, "No, it's not. It hasn't gotten cold yet."

So I like them; they're optimistic and philosophical. They're not industrialized, really—there was no industrial revolution—so they drive pretty haphazardly. They don't have a great relationship to machinery, to say the least. There's a lot of banging around and the roads are very narrow, and they just get in their cars and go, you know they just put the pedal to the metal and they're going everywhere, in all directions.

We were invited to the Scanlon estate. John Scanlon was a publicist, a very big one, in all senses of the word. He was a publicist for Bill Clinton, actually, during the Monica Lewinsky scandal, and he had this huge house in Ireland that he was inviting a group of us over to for this birthday bash. He was a big gourmand, and he perished in front of the TV after a big meal just two weeks before we were supposed to go, just died. His wife said, "Come on over anyway, John would have loved it."

So over we went, in spite of his death, about twelve of us, five children—my niece, my step-daughter, and my two sons, and Tara Newman's son—and the rest adults, and the house was big enough to accommodate that without any confusion. I have to say that this place, exqui-site stone manor that it was, reminded me a little bit of *The Shining.* It was disconcerting, ac-tually. It was set right in the middle of these woods and fields, and the kids went running in the fields with no fear of deer ticks for the first time in a long time. The woods looked like Harry Potter woods; they were very old, it was about twelve acres of land, and all very spooky.

It was in the town of Mort, which was even more of a spooky name, in the county of Offaly. O-f-f-a-l-y.

We arrived on the longest day of the year, June 21, 2001, and all went to celebrate with a treasure hunt. In the morning, the following day, the next-longest day of the year, Barbara Leary was down in the kitchen—Barbara Leary was the ex-wife of Timothy Leary and she was one of the guests there—and I was talking with her and she said that she'd dreamt that I'd done a new monologue, and I said, "No, there's nothing on the table, really, nothing new. My life is without crisis and usually they're based on crisis, and I don't have anything planned at all. Things are going smoothly."

(KNOCKS THREE TIMES ON THE DESKTOP)

So off we went to this monastery, and I guess it was kind of the first harbinger of death, although death seemed everywhere in Ireland. This was a monastery on a river where the Vikings used to come and raid it and burn the books and kill the priests. There was a funeral going on, or at least the grave diggers were digging some graves right near the monastery and taking a cigarette break. I remember that, it was kind of Hamletesque.

Then, driving home, another funereal thing happened. They had the funeral announcements on the radio. I'd never heard anything like that in my life. There must have been about sixteen deaths. Every one of them had put up a courageous struggle, had led an exemplary life, never had a bad word to say about anybody. The announcer read in a monotone, with no inflection at all, pausing about five seconds between each name and then talked about the removal time, Saturday at four-thirty, or whenever the body was going to be removed.

So there was a lot of death in the air that day. When we got home, I took a walk to kind of relieve myself of all that, and walked about six miles through dairy country. The cows were baying and mooing. Mad cow disease was around. I had a feeling they were trying to warn me about something. It was the last long walk I'd ever take in my life. I had no idea at the time, did not imagine it. At the end of the walk I came upon a calf that was in real distress. It couldn't stand up, it had arthritis, and it was looking me right in the eye and pleading with me to put it out of its pain. I told the farmer, "That calf is suffering. You should call a vet, or have something done with it." He said, "Ah, yes, I'll be doing that then. Thank you for looking after it."

So off I went thinking I'd saved the calf, or put him out of his misery, and off we went, five adults—Barbara Leary and her boyfriend, Kim;

Tara Newman; and Kathie and I—to have dinner at John Scanlon's favorite restaurant. I have to say, it wasn't that good. Maybe in terms of Irish cuisine it was, but my duck was dry.

What did we talk about—we talked about the art critic Robert Hughes's car accident that he'd had in Australia, and how difficult that would be, to have a car accident in a foreign country like that. Then there was this discussion about who would drive home. We'd all been drinking, not a lot, but Kathie had only had one glass of wine so she was the designated driver. So we're off and she says, "Buckle up," and no one in the back seat pays any attention to her. Tara Newman says, "Yes, Mom," very condescendingly, and I—God, I didn't hear her; Kathie says it's because I don't listen. I just didn't buckle up. I think I was taking a pee in the bushes, a last-minute pee, and I got in and so we're off on a backcountry road. I didn't think anything could possibly happen on a backcountry road. We'd come on a main highway and the speeding was terrific, but on the country road I thought it would be . . .

Just about one mile from the mansion—and they say these things happen within a mile of your destination, that's why my friend Donald says that he drives like crazy to get out of that radius—I look up and I see in Kathie's window what looks like a cartoon of a van. It looks like a video game. I can't take it in. We had stopped to turn right, we were still, and the road was a narrow country road, there were no lanes, just a road, and coming at me, at us, was this yellow van. It must have been coming very fast, because all I got was one glimpse of it, its headlights. It was dusk, it was ten-fifteen, and there was this enormous crash that I remember as the most violent moment of my life. It was equal to an earthquake that I'd gone through in California, which had sounded like a bomb.

Our car spun around three times, that's how hard he hit, and he drove the engine right into the front seat of the car, where Kathie burned her arm. Somehow she got out. I thought Kim, who was next to her, was dead. His forehead was down on the dashboard. Tara Newman was yelling, "The car's going to explode. Everyone get out!" I don't remember getting out, but the next I knew I was lying in the road next to Kathie, and she's saying, "I'm dying! I'm dying!" and I'm saying, solipsist that I am, "But I can't straighten out my leg!" And I couldn't. There was a woman kneeling beside me, sopping blood off my face, talking to me, saying that this is a very dangerous black spot, a black spot on the highway where there had been other accidents. She'd lost her nine-year-old son the year before just about a hundred feet from where I was lying. There was cow medicine everywhere, because the van that hit us was the veterinarian, the local vet, who, I think, probably was up taking care of that poor sick calf that I'd reported. It was bedlam. Tara Newman was directing traffic around us because none of the cars would wait. The police arrived and wouldn't even give a Breathalyzer test to the guy driving the van. They said they didn't like to get involved on that level.

The ambulance came and it took an hour. It was like a World War II bread truck, all rattling, and they loaded me in with the guy that hit me, we shared the ambulance together, and I was in such pain and shock that I did not get angry with him. To this day I regret it. I am so unconfrontational. Instead of moaning and weeping about my hip I should have been saying, "You fucking asshole! You ruined our vacation." But I'm so involved with the pain in my hip, or whatever it is that's hurting me, that I don't say anything to him at all. I'm feeling guilty because I didn't have my seat belt on. I'm feeling that it's my fault entirely.

We get to the hospital and it's run by Pakistani doctors. There's not an Irish doctor in sight, which is a little confusing for me because I suddenly feel like I'm in Pakistan. It's kind of hard to communicate. They speak English, but at the same time they don't have the same chatty bedside manner that the Irish have, at all. I was looking forward to the gift of gab to try to make me feel a little better. They're not paying any attention to Kathie, who's trying to give them advice about giving my head an MRI because I have this big bump on my head where I crashed into Kathie's head. Our heads collided and she got fourteen stitches and I got this bump. They won't do anything we request and Kathie was insisting on it and they were

having a fight with her. She was in pain because
the air bag had hit her and she had bruised
muscles around her heart. They were writing
notes on a piece of paper on her chest where
the pain was. Kathie said, "Stop it, stop it,
please. Where's your clipboard?" and the nurse
says, "Well, we don't have one."

She's taken upstairs and put in a female
dormitory, and I'm told that I have a broken
acetabulum, that I'd chipped the acetabulum
socket in my hip, and that I'd have to stay there
in the hospital for six weeks, just in traction,
and then I'd be better; I didn't need an operation. And then without any anesthesia at all
they stuck this catheter in me. It was unbeliev-
able. It made the pain of the broken hip seem
mild.

It was a country hospital and they put me in
a dormitory with five other men that are bash-
ers and crashers, mainly, I think, farmers, or

guys that have hit each other with trucks and tractors, for fun or out of drunkenness, and they're all boasting about it on their cell phones, because cell phones have taken over Ireland, as they have America. The cell phones are falling out of the bed constantly, crashing on the floor and lighting up with a little "Deet-deetle-deet-deet, deet deet," or "Be kind to your web-footed friends, for a duck may be some-body's mother." Every tune was different. I was completely disheveled because I had no paja-mas, no toothbrush. I guess you have to carry those with you, the Irish do that, in case of an accident. Kathie said that the upstairs was so dirty she had to pee in the bathtub, because the toilets were unusable.

I'm not about to stay in there for six weeks, I know that, but I don't know how to get out. I feel like a prisoner. It was a shambles in there. I had no orthopedic doctor, he was away for the weekend, so I'm in pain. They've got my foot hanging up, suspended, and they shoot me up with morphine and leave me there and in the middle of the night I woke up and hallucinated that I was in a Civil War battle, Antietam, and was wounded and was lying on a battlefield with all these other wounded soldiers around me, these other groaning farmers. I'm near the window, thank God, the window's open—you get the scent of manure, and you can hear the cows grazing and magpies cawing in the most sinister way. It all reminded me of a Brueghel painting.

The next morning is Sunday morning and the priest comes through with the Holy Eucharist and I take my first Communion, what can I tell you. I think, Why not? Then a cross-dresser comes through, I swear, out of a Fellini movie. I will never forget her, it, he. He's got long green artificial fingernails, balancing the toast between them, and he's going, "Toast! Tea! Toast!" "No, thank you, I'll pass," I said. Then a woman comes through with a clipboard, they finally found one, and she's taking a survey: Do I want the hospital to be smoke-free?

By noon the relatives of all the victims arrive with blenders and they start making daiquiris and margaritas. I wasn't offered any. They're watching the car races on television, going 192 miles an hour, and everyone is drinking. The TV is blaring, I'm alone, and oh, God, I feel a big caboose coming on. I've been constipated for two days. I call the nurse because I don't know what to do; I'm in traction, I can't get out of bed. They close the curtains and somehow, in a bedpan, they deliver this long brown snake. It's the oddest angle I've ever taken a shit at. I don't know how they do it, not batting an eye. Who would do a job like that? It was like they were delivering a baby. Then they opened the curtains and everyone just put down their forks and drinks and stared at me. I'm so excited that I get my notebook out to write about it, and the other people are looking over at me as if to say, "Oh, another James Joyce have we here? Leave it to a Yank to take a shit in the middle of lunch and then write about it."

Tara Newman arrives with the kids. Tara is in good shape. She was saved by her Prada bag. It flew up and hit the ceiling and protected her. Lucky her. I have to say, I'm a little bothered— it's awful to say this, but I'm bothered by the fact that everyone's in great spirits but I'm the only one that's injured. Kathie is recuperating very quickly upstairs. I took the brunt of it, and I don't know why. I couldn't figure out why it was me that was the chosen one, or seemed to be the chosen one, in this accident. I just got bashed in the back seat and flew around the car. I was like a missile there for a while.

Theo in all his golden innocence says, "Dad, why didn't you wear your seat belt?" and ohhhh, I didn't know what to say. I just kept reaching for my chest to try to feel the belt. Just back-seat laziness, I guess. "Now you're the real monster," he says, as he looks at my face, which is all gouged and cut. Tara looks around the hospital and goes, "Oh my God! We *did* die in the accident!"

My stepdaughter, Marissa, is there; she has to leave for the States to visit her father. She writes me a note saying, "I hope you get better. When you get back to the States I will nurse you. I know that's your fantasy."

How to get out of this place? Kathie does everything she can to get me out of there. She somehow gets ahold of the head of the Irish Arts Council, Patrick Murphy, and he was able to get in touch with a hospital outside Dublin, where they do special hip operations. The doctor there is John McElwain, and he's famous for putting together a guy that was hang gliding in the Wicklow Hills and crashed and was really in bad shape, he was Humpty Dumpty, really, and McElwain reassembled him. He's going to give me this hip operation for under a thousand dollars. It's a great deal.

Off I went in an ambulance to Taleigh. At Taleigh Hospital once again I was put in a dormitory situation, which I can't take. I'm whining, I just can't take the claustrophobia of it, in there with five other guys with their TVs all going. I don't get along with the televisions and I don't get along with most of the guys because they're all glued to the TV. I'm pleading with them to get me out of there, get me to a single room, please. They're not paying any attention, except next to me is Nicholas Dillon, who befriends me right off. He can tell that I'm upset and he gives me a Beck's nonalcoholic beer to try to get me to calm down.

Nicholas Dillon was a real hopeful guy. He lost his leg; he was a P.R. agent at a train station. He would try to help people out, that was his job, if they were lost, or find people's wallets or chase off the guys with needles that would try to rob cabs with contaminated needles instead of knives and guns. He somehow was pinned under a train that backed over him—it was a wonder it didn't kill him—and cut off the bottom of his leg from his knee down. He's got a stub. He also had a drop foot on the other leg, because the sciatic nerve was damaged. I had the same thing, my sciatic nerve was badly bruised, and they put me in a brace to keep my foot up, because it just kept dropping down. I had no control, it was flopping.

The following day they move me, because I'm complaining so much, to a single room, and

Nicholas says, "You'll be missed here." And out I go. They put me in this room with a view of a dead tree and an airshaft and a little glimpse of sky. But it's a single room and that means I don't have to listen to the TVs.

I'm in there without a television, I'm in there just reading *The Corrections.* I was making notes in my journal, that was the way I was trying to stay sane. I'm a little nervous, but it's not bad. I'm trusting this McElwain. Dr. John came in and talked with me the morning before the operation. It was all gobbledygook to me. He was going to cut open my side and go in there and see if the hip needed reinforcement, if it needed a titanium plate. If it didn't, then he'd sew me up again and that would be that.

The morning of the operation—"We're taking you to the theater today, Mr. Gray"; they're calling the operating room the theater—the anesthesiologist tries to talk me down by telling me about the glorious wars in the seventeen hundreds between England and Scotland, which I loved, because he said that's how the Grays got over from Scotland to Ireland. It was unlike the anesthesiologist in New York Hospital who tried to talk me down by asking me if I had any contacts at NYU Film School for his son.

After the operation, which they told me was successful, so I shouldn't complain, they gave me this morphine drip for forty-eight hours, and that was a treat. Every six minutes you just press this little button, and you get a shot of morphine. And I understood addiction, I'll tell you, I really understood it for the first time. With the right CDs and a view of the Wicklow Hills you wouldn't be moving from that hospital. I listened to the Grateful Dead on my stereo Walkman and became a Deadhead. I'd never been interested in them before. The morphine did it. They were playing "Touch of Gray" and the music was a ball of color with little spikes coming out of it to the different beats. It was beautiful. It was like my own little jukebox.

But after the morphine, depression set in, and I didn't know whether to discuss it with the Irish. I didn't know if they'd acknowledge the condition, or recognize it. I mean, does a fish know it's swimming in water? I had done a monologue over there called *It's a Slippery Slope,* in which I talked about divorce, depression, and skiing, and it wasn't a big hit. None of those three things were a hit in Ireland.

So I thought that I would just say I was blue.

"And why would you be blue, Mr. Gray?"

"Well, I've got a titanium plate in me I didn't have in me yesterday, and I feel like the bionic man."

"Oh, an Irishman wouldn't give it a second thought. He'd just go about his business. You Americans are too health conscious."

She's the same nurse that saw me eating raw spinach out of a plastic bag Kathie had brought, because there are no greens in the hospital.

"Ahhh, eating raw spinach, are you? Now I've seen everything!"

She's the one who found out I was an actor. "Are you in any scary movies? Because I like the scary ones."

I said, "No, not really."

"No, not *The Exorcist?*"

"No, just *The Killing Fields*, which is pretty scary."

"Oh, no, I wouldn't know anything about killing fields. Any other movies, then?"

"Oh, *Beaches.*"

"Oh, yes, what'd you play?"

"The doctor."

"Oh, sure enough, you were. Now I remember it. What's Bette Midler really like?"

"Oh, she's like herself, really. The only thing that I had problems with was when we had to do the kissing scene. She didn't want to kiss me, and I was hurt. I guess she thought I was a kiss-and-teller. Finally she did kiss me, and she said, 'All right, now I've done it. Now don't go telling the Wooster Group I kiss like Hitler.' "

Nicholas Dillon comes to visit me in his wheelchair, and he's talking about how the TVs have stolen the Irish storytelling. There just isn't the same power of the storytelling because the people aren't in the bars carrying on, they're in the bars watching television. And they're in the hospitals watching television. There's no conversation. People looked at us very suspiciously, that we were over there talking while they watched *Judge Judy*, *Ricki Lake*, and *Survivor* dubbed in Gaelic.

Kathie convinces me to rent a TV because

Wimbledon's on. But how can I watch Wimbledon when I've got this brace on my leg? What
do I want to watch a bunch of people playing
tennis for when I can't play it anymore? It's hard
for me to watch those beautiful bodies moving
so fast. I've got a drop foot from the damn accident. I can't run, I can't swim, I can't roller-blade,
I can't skate or take six-mile hikes anymore, and
I can't play tennis.

The drop foot is just numb, and the only
other person I know that has one is my friend
Mark, my old ski buddy who lives out in
Aspen, Colorado. He had an accident where he
was hanging in a tree for a night when he got
spilled by a jeep. Three other guys in it were
killed. He ended up with a drop foot and was in
and out of the hospital. He claims that the only
way I can get fixed up is to come west—the
East Coast doesn't know about drop feet—and
come to Santa Fe, where he has a healer called

Betty and the Angels. Mark's not really far out, but Betty said to put all his money into twenties and bury it for the millennium, and he did, and eat only Campbell's celery soup for months before, and he did that. So I wasn't going out there, much as I respected Mark. I thought that I would just go back to New York and try to deal with it there. I wasn't going to go to Santa Fe and I wasn't going to bury my money.

The first outing we had, Kathie took me out in a wheelchair, and I was pretty excited. We went out with the boys and we were in a construction zone with all these huge cranes around and it was depressing as all get-out. But for me it wasn't. It was beautiful. I saw the clouds at last, the horizon, the sky. I had been looking out at an air shaft for three weeks. When a bird flew across, it was a hopeful moment.

We went in, and the pinnacle of pinnacles, it was just such a treat, such a surprise, on comes the television and it's *The Simpsons,* and it's the show where Marge is yelling off-camera to Homer, who's in the bathtub with a couple of beers. Marge is saying, "Homer, come quick. The Reynolds are here and they have two extra tickets to see Spalding Gray!" And Homer goes, "I don't want to see that."

So the next day I was a little depressed.

"Depressed again, are you, Mr. Gray? Well, we should take you up to the spinal ward. There you'll see something to un-depress you."

Well, maybe I should go up there; I don't know. But I don't. Instead I visit Nicholas and his wife, Dymphia, named after the patron saint of the insane. She was one of twelve kids. "How could an intelligent country like America elect such a dud like George Bush?" Nicholas is saying. I had no answers for that one; all I could think was that America wasn't all as intelligent as Nicholas thought we were. He's raving on about this. Not exactly raving, but he says, "I wouldn't be suing for much for my leg, because we're not a litigious country like you. Did you hear about the ship that sank off the coast of America? The sharks didn't touch the lawyers out of professional courtesy."

Nicholas did have a lawyer, Bruce St. John. He came into the hospital for no charge, so I thought I'd talk with him. He was like a Dickens character, all disheveled, quoting Oscar Wilde, and had misspelled his own name on his business card. He had to white out and rewrite his name to correct it. And he wrote in some law degrees in pen on the end of the card. He was kind of making himself up as he went along. He was very jolly and up, but nothing too much about law, I would say, nothing about the case. All the stuff I really thought I loved about Ireland was happening in that hospital, the absolute chaos of it, the childlike-ness of it. Kathie had lunch with another lawyer, who said no, just stay clear of St. John, he's a little cuckoo. I didn't take him on, but I told him my whole story, passionately, and it was good to get it off my chest, as it were, but I didn't have much hope because it's all no-fault insurance there, so there wasn't any chance of collecting any money really. First it would go toward the hospitals and then what was left over, we might get a little bit.

Back in the room we play Scrabble. I'm not doing too well because I'm dyslexic and can't even turn "war" into "wart." Forrest is playing with his crash cars, and Theo is there, and Kathie looks up and sees this big dent in my forehead, where the bump was. She says, "My God, you've got a huge dent in your forehead."

I said, "Don't even say that!"

"It's so big I can stick my finger in it."

"Oh, don't say that. Call a doctor!"

The doctor comes and says, "Sure enough. It's a dent then, oh yes."

I said, "Why didn't you take an MRI? We tried to get the Pakistani doctors to take an MRI. You guys didn't take one. Why not, when I had a big bump there?"

"We're dealing with the hip. We didn't check on the head. We don't do that. We'll have to send you to another hospital."

"What one?"

"St. James. They deal with the dents there."

So they send me to St. James Hospital. I think, *Not another hospital!* In Ireland, five thousand people a year die from diseases they didn't come into the hospital with, Nicholas is telling me, frightening me with this news.

Over to St. James Hospital I go with Carmel. She's the nurse that's going to take care of me in the ambulance. In order to have this dent in my head checked out, I have to be admitted to the hospital, and the hospital for some reason has a long line of people waiting to be admitted. There are more accidents in Dublin; we don't know why. We have to do a study on that. I have some suspicions.

I was sitting there on the open breezeway in a wheelchair waiting to be admitted. Carmel is standing beside me. She is just standing. I said, "Carmel, please, please sit down."

"We are trained to stand twelve hours at a time, Mr. Gray, and this is why I'm standing."

I said, "Well, relax a bit."

"I'm fine, thank you."

Then she sees I'm cold. She takes off her sweater and puts it around me. I talk to her and ask her if she's afraid of dying.

"Oh, no."

"Will there be a priest there?"

"I don't know. I'm not exactly a practicing Catholic, because of the abortion issue."

"Why aren't you afraid of dying, then, if you won't have the priest?"

"Because the only sin is hurting someone, and I've never hurt anyone, so I'm not afraid."

"I wish I could be in that place," I say, as I look up at her all-accepting, beautiful, standing eyes. Carmel, my nurse for the day.

Forrest is there, too, supporting me with his litany of facts:

"Which can go faster, a deerfly or a cheetah?"

"How many spots on a ladybug's back?"

"Do you realize by the time I'm fifty-eight Venice will have sunk eight inches?"

I don't know where he gets this information, but he's keeping me entertained until they give me the MRI.

That is an experience because the whole room is bloody; there's blood all over the floor, there's been a horrible accident where a man and his two kids were killed, and they didn't even have time to clean up the blood. So they shuffled me in there, and the doctors afterward come out and they look like a seventh-grade geography book. They're from every part of the world except Ireland. I don't know why that bothers me but it does, because they don't have the same familiar gift of gab. Where are the Irish doctors, I'm wondering. There's an Eskimo, there's an African, there's a Pakistani, there's an Indian, a South American, and they're all conferring as to what should happen with me. They say basically I've got this open passageway, it's an orbital fracture of my eye so it's an open passageway to the brain and they simply can't have that, there's got to be an operation. Titanium plates have to be put in there or germs will get into my brain. You could get meningitis or something. It needs to be closed up.

I say, "Well, I've got to get back to the States. I can't go to another hospital."

So they start in on me. "Well, he can fly to America. You'll have the operation there."

"Oh, no, he can't. No, no, he cannot fly."

"Oh, yes, he can fly."

"Oh, no."

"Oh, yes."

"Oh, no, no, no flying." Back and forth, like this, conferring.

They finally settle and they say they'll let me out of there and I can fly back if I'm operated on immediately. Anya the nurse says, "Ah, 'tis a pity you're going. 'Tis a pity you got hit by someone the first day you're in Ireland. I hope you come back, Mr. Gray. I hope you don't hold it against us."

Noooo. I don't. I don't.

We fly back to New York, the boys in coach, Kathie and me in first class because of my leg; we had to be upgraded. The boys were good; Forrest was taking care of Theo. Forrest is a real stoic. I can remember that bike ride in the rain in Martha's Vineyard. It was similar to Ireland, it was raining—oh, my God was it raining. He rode for two hours in the rain without ever complaining once—I was bitching and moaning—until the end of the ride he just said, "Well, I hope I don't get crotch rot."

We fly over Block Island, we fly over Sag Harbor; everything was very vivid. In New York Kathie and I have sex for the first time in three weeks. I wanted to sneak in the bathroom in the hospital in Ireland, but it didn't work. When I wake up I lie in bed and I think about coincidence and fate. What if I had left my glasses in the restaurant, or my wallet, and had just gone back there. Two minutes. How many accidents had I narrowly missed because of forgetfulness? Is it sheer chance? And what does it mean that the driver of the van that hit us was named Daniel Murphy? And the real estate agent that sold our house in Sag Harbor while we were in Ireland—another calamity—was also named Daniel Murphy? And the head of the Irish Arts Council was named Patrick Murphy? Was I in the grip of some overwhelming form of Murphy's Law? I couldn't figure it out. I was getting very paranoid.

I go to New York Hospital for the operation. I'm nervous about that. Andy Warhol died there under dubious circumstances. The night before the operation I think about death. What if I die? How will the kids react? The only death in our family was Thumper, the dwarf rabbit. Kathie found him and his eyes were still open, sprawled out dead. She thought he might be faking because the vet said he was such a clever bunny. She let out with a cry when she realized that he wasn't faking. Forrest heard it upstairs and came running down, thinking it was I who had died, his dad. Kathie said, "No, it's Thumper the rabbit," and he said, "Oh." When I heard that, I kept asking Forrest, "What did you think when you thought I had died?" and he just shrugged his shoulders, "I don't know."

In the morning the orderly that takes me down to the operation is from Dublin. This is where they've all come, I guess. The operation lasts six hours. They cut me from ear to ear, peel down my forehead, and put in a titanium plate. More titanium plates in here; bone splinters are released into my frontal lobe—I think they have to try to pick those out—from the smashing of my head against Kathie's head. They sew me up; it looks like I've had a face-lift.

I have a dream that night that I'm flying over Aspen with Mark, my friend with the drop foot, and we have magic rockets on our crutches and we're going to ski. We're healed and well, and we land among the other skiers and are able to ski again. The fire alarm goes off at four A.M. and my nurse comes to tell me it's a false alarm. She just happens to be named Patricia Murphy. She's Irish. Her father was born in Tullamore, of all places, where the country hospital was where I was first in.

Is it a coincidence? I don't know. Is it fate?

Webster's Unabridged defines fate as "the power supposed to determine the outcome of events before they occur. Inevitable necessity."

Destiny: "Depending on a superior cause. Uncontrollable, according to the Stoics."

Hmm.

"Every event is determined by fate." It gives me the creeps. I don't like it. My therapist believes in such things. I wonder if I should trust her.

I've never been able to give advice before in my life. I've always been a relativist, and someone who felt that he didn't know. Even as a father it's been difficult to say what exactly one should do and should not do in this world of confusing, relativistic, movable-feast morality. But I have to say that I now can give advice around one issue, or two issues: Always wear your seat belt in the back seat of the car, which I'm sure you know, whether you do it or not. And whatever you do, get an American Express platinum card—it's only three hundred dollars extra—so you can be medevacked the *fuck* out of a foreign country if you get in an accident.

Thank you for coming tonight.

THE ANNIVERSARY

On the morning of 1/12/2000, I woke with the usual anxious feeling caused by the lingering bottom-line memory that one day, never to be known by me until I'm there, that I, as I have come to know myself, will disappear forever and ever, and ever, and forever, amen. End of story.

Kathie tried to cheer me up by reminding me that today was our tenth anniversary. That we met in Rochester ten years ago.

I don't think Kathie and I made love or had sex that morning because Theo was sleeping with us, and that always diffuses any chance for a pure, flat-out erotic event.

But on this day, January 12, 2000, I do remember the following. I remember Theo not eating his cereal. Kathie had gone to work, and I was taking care of him. I remember he quickly got bored of the TV, and wanted to play the piano with me. We did that for a while, improvising in our own way.

Then he wanted to play the Mummy with me. He had recently seen the video *The Mummy* a number of times and was most caught up by the scene in which the central character is being punished for his transgressions with the pharaoh's wife. He is being punished by being placed in a coffin and then wrapped alive like a mummy. Then the soulless pharaoh's guards turn over this large jar filled with these horrific, swarming black beetles that Theo kept referring to as "the Bees."

And these black beetles swarmed toward this poor man's head and most likely devour his living brain in a matter of seconds.

And this is what my three-year-old Theo is

most interested in having me help him reenact.
And I get to be the Mummy.

"Get in the box, Daddy, get in the box," he
says.

And I lie down on the floor and pretend to
be the Mummy.

For a moment it feels so good to be lying so
still and quiet. And then Theo releases "the
Bees." And I start screaming, to his delight.

Theo and I meet Kathie at eleven-thirty
A.M. and walk over to a nursing home on the
Lower East Side. It is at this nursing home that
Theo's godmother Freya has been vegetating
for over a year and a half from a series of
strokes she had while summering in Africa.

It is an unthinkable situation that has to be
thought about. Particularly by her daughter,
who does not, for so many apparent reasons,
does not execute her mother's living will. How

could she? Her mother talks and cries and still has a sense of humor. And she is only my age. And I am only hers.

The first time I brought Theo to see her in that nursing home his whole being went into a kind of electrified alert. The minute he entered he was all bug-eyed and looking every which way. What is this?

This time Theo is calmer. And Freya is less aware of him. She can't see, and can hardly understand how she has come to be wherever it is—she is not sure. She is in an obviously horrific bardo state. Somewhere in between living and dying. It's as if she comes alive only for visitors and then returns to some limbo state where time does not exist.

When we ask her what she thinks about she says, "Juice." She also dreams about juice. She loves to drink juice. I apologize for not bringing some. I will do it next time, I tell her.

The Anniversary

We don't stay long. We promise to return soon.

On the way out, Kathie says, "It's awful. She doesn't know what to do. She doesn't know what to feel. She doesn't deserve this. What did she do to deserve this?"

I am amazed that Kathie still seems to believe in some intrinsic justice system. Some absolute, hierarchical reward program. And at that moment I wondered if she too believed in fate.

On the way to the nursing home Kathie had told me that she had just found out that our Sag Harbor neighbor Carlos was in St. Vincent's Hospital with pneumonia. He had been in there for over a week and we hadn't gotten the message on our answering machine. The doctors didn't expect him to live. Carlos was Theo's oldest buddy, and Theo

99

was Carlos's youngest friend. We had to go right away.

When we got there we met Carlos's wife, Marie, and their daughter and her husband. They'd all been pretty much camping out at the hospital for the past week.

Carlos's wife, Marie, who is in her early seventies, was her old chatty self and very up. She was sure that Carlos was going to pull through, even though the doctors only gave him a one percent chance. Marie was so enthusiastic about the emergency room and all the nurses that she wanted to give me her own tour right away, starting with the four-hundred-pound Egyptian who was also lying in bed with pneumonia.

She told me how it took six men to carry him in. I peeked in at him, or rather at the massive bulk of bedding I took to be him. A small woman I took to be his wife was kneeling and praying over his giant body.

The Anniversary

When I at last came to Carlos, with all those tubes coming out of him, I really didn't know what to say, but I felt I had to say something. Marie told me he was not conscious, but I thought he might still be able to hear me. I said, "Hi, Carlos. It's Spalding. I hope you get better soon."

I wish I had had a new joke to tell him, but I didn't. I don't remember any jokes, except for the one Carlos told me. The one that goes, "A skeleton walked into a bar, and ordered a glass of beer and a mop."

Outside in the waiting room, Marie told me that there were people all over the world praying for Carlos. She also told me that if I needed any kindling to start my fire at home, to look in their driveway because Carlos had left a pile of sticks there for me. Was that where his life had stopped?

Going down on the elevator with Kathie and Theo, I thought, Why not pray for Carlos? It might be better than just standing here waiting for the elevator to reach the first floor. I didn't know how to pray or who to pray to, so I just did the first thing that came to mind. I imagined myself standing at the end of Carlos's bed. I visualized a warm ball of energy at the base of my spine. It looked like a little sun. Then I let it rise up my spine and burst out the top of my head. It burst out like a volcano of multicolored confetti, and it sprayed up and out and settled on Carlos like a colorful electric snow. Like a sixties poster, I thought, and at the same time I wondered why I hadn't prayed for my dad when he was dying in the hospital.

Outside, on the street, Kathie asked me if I had cried when I saw Carlos. "No," I said. "Did you?" "Yes," she said, "I couldn't help it."

The Anniversary

On the sidewalk outside St. Vincent's, Kathie suggested that I take Theo to ride on the carousel in Central Park. "What a great idea," I said. "I am so glad you thought of that."

Theo and I took a cab to Fifty-ninth Street and Sixth Avenue. I couldn't stand to look out the window at the city, so I watched Theo watching the city. I never took my eyes off him for the whole trip.

Once we got to the park, Theo got very involved with all the natural rock outcroppings. I had never realized how real they were until I saw him playing on them. Before this day, they had always seemed somewhat artificial in my mind. I hadn't realized how big they were and how many there were between Fifty-ninth Street and the carousel.

Theo seemed to feel no need to get to the merry-go-round. He was happy just climbing on the rocks. But I, who thought I really wanted to make it to the carousel before it closed, kept saying, "C'mon, Theo, don't you want to ride on the horsies?"

We arrived at the carousel just a few minutes before it was to close. There was a man already slamming down some of the sliding metal doors. Oh, what a violent sound.

We were the only ones on the merry-go-round and it was going very fast. Theo was on an outside horse, and I was on the horse just in from him. I looked over at Theo going up and down to the music and I saw that he was very, very happy. He was purely, utterly, very happy. There was no room for anything else but the happiness that filled him.

I don't remember who did it first, but . . . no, it was me . . . or was it I? Anyway, I let out with a yell that was sort of half performed and half spontaneously real. In other words, I was quite aware of it coming out of me and how it sounded. And I do know that it was my yell that triggered Theo, and he just lifted his head back and let out with this yelping, joyful cry. It was like out of a movie, only better. His cry just grabbed the whole day by the feet, by the short hairs, and gathered it up. It was pure celebration. It was unadulterated happiness.

That one ride was enough for both of us, and anyway it was clear they were closing the carousel down. Then, on my way out, Theo spotted "the treats." There was a little display of gum and candy at convenient child level, right on our way out. Theo seemed to know exactly what he wanted. It was what they call a "ring pop." A sort of candy pacifier. A plastic ring with a giant, glassy, ruby-red candy shaped like a Walt Disney diamond.

I picked up the ring pop and looked around but didn't see anyone handy to pay. So I just dropped it into my pocket. I'd never done any-thing like that before, or at least not often, and I didn't give it a second thought.

As we were leaving, the man closing the metal doors turned and said, "What about that candy, mister?" I was taken completely by sur-prise. "Oh, this?" I said, pulling out the ring pop from my pocket. "What do I owe you?"

"That's fifty cents."

Then he suddenly changed his mind and said, "No, give it back. We are closed here now."

I watched Theo watch me give the ring pop back to the man. Theo was incredulous, but at the same time seemed confused and intimi-dated by the power of the situation. What was wrong, he wondered, more than he needed that candy.

"Why, Dad? Why the guy say that?"

"None of us want you to eat so much candy, Theo," I said as I walked briskly up the path, pulling Theo by the hand. Behind us, the carousel man was making a fist with his hand and yelling after us, "Your son is going to end up in prison one day!"

At the top of the hill, just beyond the carousel, I could see the rows of American elms, catching the last of the day's light. They were all dark and twisting and casting incredible shadows on the green lawn. Should the grass be this green in January? I wondered as I sat down with Theo to gaze at my favorite place in Central Park. These trees, these trees, these beautiful trees.

As soon as we sat down, Theo asked for his bottle, and I pulled it out of my pocket and gave it to him. Then he leaned his head against my body while he sucked. While he drank.

On the way to the subway, every time I saw a cop, I saw the headlines:

MONOLOGUIST AND THREE-YEAR-OLD SON
CAUGHT RED-HANDED—TALK YOUR WAY OUT
OF THIS ONE, MR. SPALDING

Theo and I took the A train home. On the subway I tried thinking about the words "fate," "necessity," and "chance." I kept trying to put "necessity" and "sacred" together. I thought also about how I could not imagine living without my children, and how I would either have to die or learn to live without them. I thought about my mother and how she couldn't live without us, and how she took the more extreme way out. I thought about how none of this day would have been had I not gone alone to P.S. 122 to see the avant-garde-drama that fateful night in November of 1989, where, while watching Frank Maya perform, I was tapped on the shoulder by Larry Champoux, who just happened to be Kathie Russo's boss at the Pyramid Arts Center in Rochester, New York.

"How would you like to come up and perform your stuff at our space?" he asked me.

"Sure, why not?" I said. "Here's my phone number—give me a call."

And he did.

And I went.

And Kathie Russo picked me up at the airport.

DEAR NEW YORK CITY

Dear New York City,

For thirty-four years I lived with you and came to love you. I came to you because I loved theater and found theater everywhere I looked. I fled New England and came to Manhattan, that island off the coast of America, where human nature was king and everyone exuded character and had big attitude. You gave me a sense of humor because you are so absurd.

When we were kids, my mom hung a poster over our bed. It had a picture of a bumblebee, and under the picture the caption read:

According to all aerodynamic laws, the bumblebee cannot fly, because its body weight is not in the right proportion to its wingspan. But ignoring these laws, the bee flies anyway.

That is still New York City for me.

Though nothing can bring back the hour

Of splendor in the grass, of glory in the flower;

We will grieve not, rather find

Strength in what remains behind.

—William Wordsworth

CELEBRATING THE LIFE OF
SPALDING GRAY

VIVIAN BEAUMONT THEATER
LINCOLN CENTER
NEW YORK

April 13, 2004

Laurie Anderson was born in Chicago. The experimental attitude of many young artists in downtown New York fostered by the art scene of the early 1970s attracted her, and some of her earliest performances took place on the street or in informal art spaces. Since then, she has gone on to create large-scale theatrical works that combine a variety of media. As a visual artist, her work has been shown at the Guggenheim Museum in SoHo, as well as extensively in Europe, including at the Centre Georges Pompidou in Paris. She has also released seven albums for Warner Bros. In 1999 she staged *Songs and Stories from Moby Dick*, an interpretation of Herman Melville's 1851 novel. She lives in New York.

Laurie Anderson

I knew Spalding for many years and would often see him out on the road around America. Since we often traveled on the same circuits, we'd hang out in coffee shops and greenrooms and complain about how horrible it was to be on the road, and how much fun it was. I wrote the music for a couple of Spalding's films, *Swimming to Cambodia* and *Monster in a Box*, so I listened to recordings of him for hours on end, and I really got to know more and more about the ways that he loved the world and language and how he looked at people and cities and, again and again, his dreams, his so many dreams, and his visions, and his search, of course, for the perfect moment. Because he was an artist who really understood time and what a total illusion it is. He was also, of course, a master of sense of timing, which often made painful things very hilarious just by putting them together just so.

Now, it was my job to set all of this to music. And one of the things music can do is tell you how to feel. It can cue emotion. It can make a shot of a rose seem really ominous or triumphant. Spalding's movies, on the one hand, were physically a glass of water on a table and a microphone, but really were enormous paintings of the world and, of course, his voice. And inside his voice were a million things, and none of them simple. He could be sly and ridiculous and profound all at once, in the same moment. He didn't really need music, although I did give some music to him anyway. But when I think of him now I think of his love for the world and his effort to really pay attention to it and to open his eyes.

Celebrating the Life of Spalding Gray

I'd like to read a short poem that I really love by a great artist and another great writer, Allen Ginsberg. It's a poem about love, supposedly a love poem. It's called "Song."

(READING OF "SONG" BY ALLEN GINSBERG)

John Perry Barlow is a former Wyoming rancher and Grateful Dead lyricist. More recently, he cofounded and still cochairs the Electronic Frontier Foundation. He has written for many publications, including the *New York Times* and *Time,* and has been on the masthead of *Wired* magazine since it was founded. In 1997 he was a Fellow at Harvard's Institute of Politics, and since 1998 he has been a Berkman Fellow at Harvard Law School. He writes, speaks, and consults on a broad variety of subjects, particularly digital economy. He lives in Wyoming, New York, and San Francisco and has three teenage daughters.

John Perry Barlow

*When I first heard that Spalding had disap-*peared, I knew. But there is an expert part of my nature, the denial part, that immediately began ginning up an alternative explanation.

I imagined him actually attempting a swim to Cambodia. I saw him swan-diving from the rail of the Staten Island Ferry, rounding Sandy Hook by dawn, and turning south for Cape Horn. What a great monologue this is going to make, I thought. Or not. Spalding inhabited a magical reality where such feats might actually be possible.

In my less magical reality, it was easier to see him beneath all that black water. He'd been under a darkness as cold and opaque for some time. I've had my low moments, and I'd seen plenty of his over the years, but I have never been in the presence of a depression so leaden, nor a monomania so circular as what wrapped itself around the soul of Spalding Gray in September 2001. From the time it got him until the time he dove, his life was a purgatory of uselessness, barren of joy and meaning. Love, incoming or outgoing, became something he could think but not feel. I don't blame him for what he did. He hung tough with it longer than I could have.

The brain can be a cruel organ. When it breaks, it breaks the universe.

Given the pall of his two last years, coupled with his more theatrical previous miseries, it's easy to forget how happy Spalding was for most of the '90s. He embraced the wholesome life with weird ease. He became a devoted family man who loved Forrest, and Theo, and

Kathie, and Marissa even more than he loved suffering. From the moment he stepped up to fatherhood, back in '93, he was a passionate, if unorthodox, dad. And he was delighted to be one until all his delight was surgically removed in a hospital on the Upper East Side in September 2001.

In addition to his strange fitness as a father, Spalding was a man of many ironies. Of these, I think the greatest was his selfless generosity of spirit, improbable in a professional narcissist. He gave us *himself*, as he was, flawed and naked before our judgment. In doing so, he extended a healing permission to us. Being utterly disclosed before strangers creates a zone of general amnesty that loosens the shackles of everyone's quiet desperations. It is a blow against the pursuit of loneliness.

With this gift, Spalding changed people's lives, profoundly and often. This has been made very clear to me in the last few months. When Spalding disappeared, I posted something to my weblog about it. An extraordinary bloom of sweet commentary has arisen in response. As of this morning, there have been 572 tributes to Spalding posted to my blog. Another 728 e-mails have been sent to me personally. Five megabytes of strange beauty.

These memoria are long, eloquent, and achingly honest. I wish I had time to quote from them here. They are filled with tales of suicide attempted, depression and madness endured, and joy fully experienced. Nearly every one contains a perfect moment or two. They demonstrate the spreading contagion of his candor and his raconteur's genius for investing ordinary details with more universal magic.

He was certainly not afraid to talk to strangers, so I'm not quite surprised by how many of these folks relate deeply personal encounters with Spalding. That his own quirky voice and viewpoint is woven so discernibly into theirs seems proof that the soul is not so easily contained by its original bottle of flesh. Though widely distributed, there may be more of Spalding in the world now than there was when he was still walking around muttering to himself.

These people, and we here today, are his witnesses. We are collective evidence that Spalding planted something beautiful, if a little goofy, among us. It is a holy thing. It will continue to blossom even without his being here to tend it. Death doesn't have Spalding Gray. We do.

Joe Berlinger is an award-winning filmmaker and jour-
nalist. His films include *Brother's Keeper, Paradise Lost:
The Child Murders at Robin Hood Hills, Revelations: Paradise
Lost 2,* and *Metallica: Some Kind of Monster,* among many
other film and television projects. His first book,
Metallica: This Monster Lives, the inside story of the
making of the Metallica film, was recently published
by St. Martin's Press.

Joe Berlinger

*Hi, I'm Joe Berlinger and I'm a documentary film-*maker, not a public speaker, so I'm a little terrified right now, but Spalding was such a personal and professional inspiration to me as someone who explores the human condition. I found him to be very inspiring in my own work, and also he was a great friend, so I'm going to overcome my personal demons here and talk.

I met Spalding in 1992 at the Sundance Film Festival. My filmmaking partner, Bruce Sinofsky, and I had just finished our first film called *Brother's Keeper,* and we were lucky enough to win the Audience Award, which was a big honor for a first film, and Spalding was the awards presenter. He was very excited about the film and in fact when he presented us with the award he told this great story that I still laugh at. Basically he talked about how he could not tear himself away from watching *Brother's Keeper* even though he desperately had to take a leak. He had too much water, too much coffee in the morning and desperately had to pee, but found the film so exhilarating and so meaningful that it was the first movie he ever sat through having to take a pee. And this was the story that he told when he gave us the award. It was very Spalding, because all in one ball it summed up the humor and the intelligence and the wit and the deep exploration that this man was all about.

That was our encounter, but four months later, five months later, we thought we were going to get a big distribution deal from winning the Audience Award. Of course, every distributor on both coasts passed on the movie, didn't think it would do any theatrical business. My partner Bruce and I decided that we were going to get this movie into theaters come hell or high water, so we started our own little distribution company not knowing anything about distribution and we were well into our plans and the movie was about to open in about two months and all of a sudden Bruce and I panicked because we realized we didn't have a movie trailer, a coming attractions trailer. All of a sudden for whatever reason I flashed on the pee story from Sundance. I called up Spalding and I said, "Hey, Spalding, remember us? You gave us an award. You loved our movie. We'd love you to do a monologue about having to take a leak at Sundance while watching our movie, and in fact, we're going to make movie trailer history without any footage from the film." Because our negative for the movie was tied up at the lab—we were doing a 16mm to 35mm blowup—we had no negative, we had no game plan other than we were going to film Spalding telling the pee story. I figured he would give me all sorts of reasons why he couldn't do it, but with the same enthusiasm that he presented us the award with, he embraced it. In fact, I have the trailer and I'd like to show it to you because this is how I want to remember Spalding.

(TRAILER FOR *BROTHER'S KEEPER*)

Over the years, from that, Spalding was a huge supporter of our work, came to every premiere we had since then. Eventually my wife and Kathie hit it off at the *Paradise Lost* premiere and our families spent a lot of time together up in Brewster, mainly. This is the Spalding I remember—a man of great compassion, wit, intelligence. The Spalding who came back from

Ireland was a damaged man. We who have had decades or longtime experience with him remember him this way. I think it's very important for Theo and Forrest and Marissa to remember that this is the Spalding we all know and love. The man who came back damaged was Spalding, of course, but it wasn't the person who was so inspiring to so many people around the world. I hope you remember that.

Eric Bogosian writes plays, solos, and books. Every now and then he acts in something. His best-known plays (both of which were made into films) are *Talk Radio* (in which he starred and received the Berlin Film Fest Silver Bear Award) and *subUrbia*. Between 1980 and 2000 he created six full-length solos (*Sex, Drugs, Rock & Roll, Pounding Nails in the Floor with My Forehead,* et al.), garnering three Obies and a Drama Desk Award. His most recent solo, *Wake Up and Smell the Coffee,* was released on DVD in 2004, and earlier in 2005 Theater Communications Group published a collection of his plays (*Humpty Dumpty and Other Plays*), and Simon & Schuster published his second novel, *Wasted Beauty*. Bogosian is the recipient of a 2004 Guggenheim Fellowship.

Eric Bogosian

I first met Spalding Gray in 1975 when I was a theater student working as a gopher at the Chelsea Westside Theater. I had come down to SoHo to see "experimental theater" and the Wooster Group was on my list. They were performing Sam Shepard's *Tooth of Crime.* Spalding originated the role of Hoss and was on the cover of the Grove Press edition of the play, so from my perspective he was a major star. After the performance, I asked him if he would let me buy him a cup of coffee and he said yes, so we wandered off to Magoo's, the watering hole of the day, and we talked. I wish I could remember what we talked about, I'm sure it was historic, but it was probably the usual "keep your nose to the grindstone" stuff that older theater people tell younger theater people so they won't get discouraged by the harsh truth. I do remember that he was interested in me and very supportive and enthusiastic, which meant a lot to me. The encouragement stuck with me and I'll always be grateful for that cup of coffee.

Hanging with me was typical of Spalding because Spalding had a voracious appetite for people and for experience. Of course, that afternoon, he and I had no idea that over the next twenty years we would be linked because we would both go on to focus on solo work and because we would perform in the same theaters and share a number of friends. In fact, we toured the same circuit around the U.S. I would often get to a city after Spalding had left and the presenters would regale me with tales of all the cool things Spalding did while he was there. I'd hear about how Spalding went skiing or dancing or skeet-shooting, whatever. This was in stark contrast to my hermetic behavior on the road in which I check in and hang the DND sign on my door and watch nature shows on PBS until it's time to go onstage.

In a way, and he said so himself, he saw his life as material for his solos. He did things so he could tell us stories.

I think I saw one of the first, if not the first, solo at DTW. It was exhilarating, because I knew that Spalding was going to sit down and try to hold the audience for over an hour with no script. And he pulled it off. It was electric. There was no attempt at that time at humor or entertainment. It was an experimental theater piece predicated on an idea, like his piece *Interviewing the Audience.* He didn't know where it was going to go; he liked the danger.

By his last solo at P.S. 122, which I also attended, he had become the grand raconteur, the master storyteller. In twenty years Spalding had covered a lot of ground. Many of us know more about the details of his life than we know about famous people in history, or our own relatives. He was not strictly an autobiographer, rather a diarist, building his solos out of the minutiae, rather than the historically significant elements, in his life. And he was making genuine theater pieces, plays for one person, evidenced by the fact that each solo had a point, a theme. In his best pieces, the underlying idea would be unforgettable, as in the "perfect moment" moment in *Swimming to Cambodia*. Spalding understood that art is not about truth but about invention. That this incident plus that incident, told in the right way, invents a storyline for a life, a thematic center. An angle. It was not just the incidents that Spalding gave us, but the angles. The attitudes. Spalding told inspirational stories, stories about life lessons. That's why we dug him.

His work went beyond entertainment. We knew from his work with Liz LeCompte, particularly in the Rhode Island Trilogy, that there was a dark shadow in Spalding's past, and this tragic aspect informed the deadpan humor of his solos. We watched him buck himself up with irony and laughter, as if to make it through another day. What was genuinely frightening to him in real life—for instance, flying on an airplane—he transformed into humor. He took the anarchy and the illogic of life and molded it into something we could grab hold of. In a way, Spalding was forever struggling and he presented this struggle to us onstage. During the performances, he let us walk in his shoes, or skis, or whatever. And so we experienced what he experienced, with all the ups and downs, and the effect was often magical.

I want to say this today: It took courage to do this. Courage to make theater so naked and unadorned, courage to expose himself in this way, and courage to fight his demons in public. In so doing he entered our hearts, my heart, because he made his struggle my struggle, his life became my life.

I have received phone calls, notes, and e-mails from people expressing their feelings on Spalding's passing. The one that moved me the most simply said, "So sad to hear the news about Spalding Gray. It is a great loss." It *is* a great loss. I am very sad that I will no longer hear what Spalding has to say about his and my life.

Bernard Gersten has been the Executive Producer of Lincoln Center Theater since its reestablishment in 1985. He was producer of the NBC documentary film *Voices of Sarafina!* and served as associate producer of the New York Shakespeare Festival, executive vice president of Zoetrope Studios, executive producer of Francis Ford Coppola's *One from the Heart*, and coproducer of the live orchestra presentations throughout the world of Able Gance's *Napoleon*. He was the vice president of Radio City Music Hall and executive producer of *Porgy and Bess* and *Ice*.

Bernard Gersten

This theater remembers Spalding. It's in the bricks and in our bones. You can look into Spalding's wistful eyes peering at passersby in the lower lobby mural. Playwrights, directors, designers, actors, stage managers, musicians, technicians, everyone who works at the Mitzi Newhouse or here at the Beaumont, those who come to audition, those who visit backstage after performances encounter Spalding in six separate locations along the dressing room corridors where large wall-size posters recall the seven shows Spalding did here.

2.

Spalding was a big part of the early years of Lincoln Center Theater with his repertoire of performances that began in the Mitzi Newhouse—somewhat hesitantly—the theater being located, as it is, well north of 14th Street. Spalding needed convincing that he "belonged" uptown. The ultimate persuasion was getting him to act in his first Broadway play— the part of the stage manager—in Lincoln Center Theater's production of *Our Town*, outstandingly directed by Gregory Mosher at the Lyceum Theatre. Spalding was extraordinary, and the production won the Tony for Best Revival, in no small measure thanks to Spalding's notable performance.

Spalding's early monologues were in the three-hundred-seat Mitzi Newhouse where he did *Terrors of Pleasure, Sex and Death to the Age 14,* and *Swimming to Cambodia.*

3.

Doing six shows a week was a tough, demanding schedule. When it was pointed out to Spalding that he could play to more people in two nights at the Beaumont than in six nights at the Mitzi, he came up here and scoped out the hall. It looked awesome at first; he was uncertain that he could encompass the audience that circled all the way to his left and all the way to his right. Or that he could get through to a thousand people gathered in one room. But the idea of working two nights a week instead of six carried the day, and Spalding decided to give it a try with *Monster in a Box*. From the moment he walked onstage to be enthusiastically greeted by a thousand pairs of clapping hands, soon followed by the resounding roll of his first laugh, Spalding knew he was home free, and for *Monster, It's a Slippery Slope*, and *Morning, Noon and Night* the Beaumont was his uptown home.

4.

Spalding's seven works were of a piece with the one hundred and three productions that Lincoln Center Theater produced here, in the Newhouse and elsewhere over the last nineteen years. The wonder was that Spalding, all by himself, sitting at that table, the text at his fingertips, could hold the audience in equal thrall with productions requiring the ministrations of dozens of actors, countless musicians, stagehands, scenery, and costumes galore. But Spalding, *all by himself*, satisfied Shakespeare's injunction to the players to "hold as 'twere the mirror up to nature." The nature that Spalding mirrored may have been his own, but in that deep reflection we found ourselves as well. And that was what made Spalding's work such full-bodied, irresistible theater.

5.

When we heard that Spalding was at work on his post-Ireland installment of his life as art and that there were to be performances last winter at P.S. 122, we arranged tickets, with high hopes that he would feel ready for the Beaumont by about this time and might perhaps be playing in rep with Christopher Plummer's powerful King Lear. Word came back that Spalding felt he wasn't up to being seen yet and could we hold off for a while.

Well, we held off. And here we are today remembering in sorrow and with a painful sense of loss the Spalding we knew, loved, and oh so deeply miss.

Suzanne Gluck, co-head of the William Morris Agency Book Department, was Spalding Gray's literary agent for twenty years.

Suzanne Gluck

Spalding Gray was my first client. Who but Spalding would walk through the door to a windowless office with no books on the shelves and never think to ask, "Who else do you represent?" And so our relationship began, our trust in each other blind and immediate.

It was soon clear to me that for a self-proclaimed neurotic, Spalding was remarkably courageous. From his penchant for swimming in the middle of the ocean, to undergoing psychic surgery in the Philippines, to learning to ski black diamonds at age fifty, he clearly never saw a door he didn't try to walk through. Even a car door. He was once famously mistaken for a Bowery bum by three Hasidic Jews looking for a Sunday sweeper for their Williamsburg temple. Rather than explain the error, he did a wonderful job and earned ten dollars.

He was an unconventional author, to say the least. As in so many things, Spalding was out ahead of the world. He was the first author to publish his personal storytelling, and ironically, through his own extraordinary gift, he made us all feel that our own stories were important, paving the way for everyone from his fellow monologuists to the offbeat memoirs that everyone seems to write now.

Despite a chosen profession of public speaking, no one loved listening to other people's stories as much as Spalding, a fact that always surprised people in publishing. "Stories seem to fly to me and stick." That's the first line of the preface to the book *Sex and Death to the Age 14*. "They are always out there, coming in. We exist in a fabric of personal stories. So I never wonder whether, if a tree falls in the forest, will anyone hear it. Rather, who will tell about it?"

However, it was parenthood that finally got Spalding talking easily in private. In fact it was almost shocking to hear him, a "regular dad," fall into an everyday kind of small talk. He was particularly fond of describing how Forrest, as a very young boy, was able to feel truly satisfied with what he had, leaving toy stores empty-handed and giving away his Halloween candy to other trick-or-treaters. This was his new trove of stories to mine, those of his own children, and he never tired of telling them.

When I picture him now, a scene comes to mind: after a summer dinner, on the porch of his house in Carmel, dancing to the radio with Marissa and Forrest and Theo, a part of no performance, free of every thought that was not dancing in the twilight with the children he loved so much. The only story at that moment, the happy story of his life.

Primarily a stage actress, *Lee Grant* has also been distinguished for her feature film and television work. The daughter of an actress and model, Grant was only four when she debuted in a show at the Metropolitan Opera. She joined the American Ballet at age eleven, graduated from high school at fourteen, and received a scholarship to the Neighborhood Playhouse. She won a Critics Circle Award for her role in the 1949 Broadway production *Detective Story* and earned an Oscar nomination and the Cannes Festival's Best Actress award for the 1951 film version. Her promising film career was abruptly derailed when she refused to testify before the House Un-American Activities Committee and was promptly blacklisted. Although her stage career thrived, it would be twelve years before Grant would be able to get substantial roles in television or movies. She became a director in 1980 with the moving *Tell Me a Riddle.* Subsequent directorial efforts include *A Matter of Sex* (1984) and *Reunion* (1994).

Lee Grant

Long ago, before Spalding fell in love with Kathie, and before Spalding became a dad, he would show up at our apartment on New Year's Eve. Together we shed many of the past years, and together we faced the fear and excitement of the new one. The coming together of wondrous people for one night. Spalding was wondrous. He was kind, he was warm, and he had a mysterious, raging talent. I celebrate his humanity and his life with you.

This is from Whitman.

I depart as air, I shake my white locks at
   the runaway sun,
I effuse my flesh in eddies, and drift it in
   lacy jags.

I bequeath myself to the dirt to grow from
    the grass I love,
If you want me again look for me under
    your boot-soles.

You will hardly know who I am or what I
    mean,
But I shall be good health to you
    nevertheless,
And filtre and fibre your blood.

Failing to fetch me at first keep
    encouraged,
Missing me one place search another,
I stop somewhere waiting for you.

Robert Holman is a poet (most recent book: *A Couple of Ways of Doing Something*, a collaboration with Chuck Close), performer (most recent CD: *In with the Out Crowd*), producer (*The United States of Poetry* for PBS), professor (Visiting Professor of Writing at Columbia University), and proprietor (Bowery Poetry Club).

Robert Holman

Night of the Living Dead Every Day

Help Me

I Can See

—sign on Pedro Pietri's begging can*

Spalding and I in *No Exit*. He is just dead
as I am age 56 today, living. "Sartre says,"
   Spalding says
"Buñuel," continue I, *"Exterminating Angel"*
To die in water, to be hauled to air
I walk the earth fair who cares

---

*Please send synonyms. "Begging can" is awkward but true—
a Bustelo tin painted black with white vinyl letters applied.
Please do not send "alms basket"—pretty but a lie.

Celebrating the Life of Spalding Gray

"It is spring again, I wonder
why," as James Schuyler once said
wrote to no one
in particular and always
the empty chair and table with full glass

What can I say
write? Swimming
upstream to Green
Point, the icy flow and corduroy
ferrying home. You can't
sleep with the fishes cause
the fishes don't sleep as Nick
Jones says
sings. Spuddy's solid strokes pulling
even with his dragging foot
and head plate, towing me
to shore where we rest for a while.

As I was saying and saying
I was saying as and as I was

and as I was saying what I
was saying was what I was

The doors and windows of Romero's
Night of the Living Dead conveniently
open in one direction but they open
and the zombies are everywhere. Spalding

is dancing with them, Buddha doing a soft
shoe round the empty chair on the empty
   table
brandishing the full glass and I am trying
to write it down down
like time sinks. "Good line!" tosses
   Spalding over
his shoulder. Then, "Who can rhyme
sublime with sublime and love with
doubt's the bottom line?" He whoops,
red-faced & leering ecstatic and never
dead, straight into his name.

Celebrating the Life of Spalding Gray

Now we are here forever someone
   mentions (OK, me)
trying to make the lines that add
up not
down dissolving chair into table all into
   glass

Only I am breathing. "Awfully
parochial," says my man Spalding
who is talking so fast I can't write it pure
sound highest-speed synapse crackle
"I can't sleep I can't sleep" sings
Spalding remembering everything

Just a couple more: how ancestors become
   family
causing to escape the word Happiness
which will be poem with no metaphors
   allowed

not one word poem but one life poem
as zombies
scale the walls in Sag Harbor
busting in as the room breathes
axes in the windows they are singing
Happy Birthday to you, surprise,
but the words are Auld Lang Syne

what was I saying what I
was saying was what I was

A. M. Homes is the author of the novels *Music for Torching*, *The End of Alice*, *In a Country of Mothers*, *Jack*, and a collection of stories, *The Safety of Objects*. Among her many awards are Guggenheim and NEA fellowships. Homes is a contributing editor to *Vanity Fair* and has published fiction and essays in *The New Yorker*, *Granta*, *McSweeney's*, *Art Forum*, and the *New York Times*. She lives in New York City.

A. M. Homes

I met Spalding on one of the first days of my adult life. I was a transfer student at Sarah Lawrence College—it was the first week of school, I knew no one. Adrienne Rich was coming to give the big back-to-school reading, and the same night there was an event scheduled—part of a series on performance art curated by one of the students. That performance was Spalding Gray's *A Personal History of the American Theatre.*

Well, I loved the theater, I liked to think I was sort of a theater person, I'd worked the lights in high school, taken a summer course in the musical with Josh Logan, written plays, and so, while all the students flocked into the big auditorium to hear the iconic poet, I went down into a small basement room. There was a plain wooden desk, a glass of water, a box of cards. A man in a plaid shirt came out, took a sip of water, said, "I'm not Adrienne Rich"—a couple of people left immediately. He took another sip of water and began.

Spalding became an invisible mentor, a big brother. The next year I was in Washington, D.C., and Spalding was there on an extended residency. I went to the theater every night. There was a plain wooden table like a school desk with its Shaker simplicity; the uniform, a patrician plaid shirt; the spiral-bound notebooks he carried with him like a schoolboy about to deliver his report. I watched the notebooks, wondering what was in them. Was every line written out point by point? Or was it filled with a general outline, concepts, or perhaps they were blank, just a prop? I could never bring myself to ask, or peek.

He was a one-man band, a psychosocial anthropologist, excavating his mind, contemplating the collective navel, with a supporting cast of thousands. This was the collective experience, the ethos and pathos of our time.

I had conversations with Spalding that I couldn't have with anyone else; nothing was too weird to tell him. He would find a detail, a fine point, and peel it back, opening the subject further and further, pulling out the macrocosm within the microcosm.

His was a quest for truth, for clarity, a determination to stay faithful to the story—and he was the story.

He needed to believe, to experience everything intimately and in its entirety, to know pain and joy and the extremes of each. Obsessed with the everyday, questing for normal, his was a struggle to make order, to transcend, to transform banality into sublime experience.

Back in Washington years ago, I went out for breakfast with Spalding on Mother's Day. He talked about his family, growing up a Christian Scientist, about his mother, about death.

As he was talking about his mother's suicide, he was also telling me that he was convinced that the waiters at this particular restaurant were poisoning him, and yet he went there every day, it was the only place he would go. They were poisoning him, but he liked the food and what did that mean?

He was afraid of everything, but the more afraid he was the more he charged forward, hurling himself toward the anxiety.

He lived in terror of life itself. There was a porousness to his humanity, a primal vulnerability that let him be profoundly affected by anything and everything.

His relationship with death was such that it

was ever-present, friend and foe, a comfort and an inescapable temptation, waiting in the wings.

For Spalding each thing led to the next, that was how he navigated, moving from obsession to obsession, constantly finding connections, meanings that would lead him from thing to thing, Spalding and the novel, Spalding and the house upstate, Spalding and his eyes, Spalding and the birth of his children.

Always and inescapably Spalding spinning stories, magical tales, transcendent, luminescent.

In his life with Kathie and Marissa, Forrest and Theo he found something he'd never had before—contentment.

When Spalding went missing, I comforted myself with the idea that if anyone could disappear and come back it would be Spalding. I could imagine him making a pilgrimage back to Rhode Island, could imagine him needing to go on his own version of a walkabout, could see him observing his life from afar, imagine him needing to know what life would be like without him, seeing, knowing that it would go on—finding comfort there, and knowing how much he would be missed.

It never dawned on me how famous Spalding was until he disappeared.

Articles appeared in newspapers around the world, articles and then editorials, blogs in which people told stories of their experiences with Spalding: loaning him their apartments so he'd have a place to sleep after a show, running into him on a nude beach in California, dancing with him in a bar. How deeply they identified with his incredibly personal stories; they saw themselves in Spalding.

Right now as we are gathering here, people are gathering in other cities, hosting their own memorials.

Spalding's death is the fateful combining of

history, biology, and an accident. Is there making sense of it? Is there closure? There is something in the recognition that it could have been any of us, something in the sharing of these memories, in noting how many people were touched by Spalding, in the very real presence of each of you who are here today.

In all of this I have waited for the epiphanic moment, the big *aha* that will put it together; there is the desire to make sense out of life, to have it add up to, for there to be greater meaning.

If one wanted to be poetic, we could go back to the water, the importance of the water, the fluidity and constancy.

And then there is the plaid shirt, the plain wooden table, the carefully sipped glass of water.

It was never that life wasn't enough—it was that life was too much.

Roger Rosenblatt's essays for print and for television have won two George Polk Awards, the Peabody, and the Emmy, among others. The author of ten nonfiction books and four plays, his first novel will be published in 2006.

Roger Rosenblatt

He said that you can't be present in the place you're in until you've left and want to go back.

He also said his two favorite Dollies were Parton and Lama.

Spalding the hilarious. Spalding the self-exposed, the puzzled, the scared, the brave. Spalding the supporting actor. That's what he was in the movies. But as an artist, he changed the whole idea of what a supporting actor is. He supported us. He played our part—we who wish to think we're the stars of the show, but who, in our shaky, collapsible hearts, know better, and yet also know that we have a certain significance, that we definitely are.

Spalding was the supporting actor who was

also the star. Man as supporting actor. In *Swimming to Cambodia*, he said, "When I was in therapy about two years ago, one day I noticed that I hadn't any children." It was the perfect statement of the star in the supporting role—as if he has just noticed he was onstage at all, much less center stage.

As to the substance of that observation: Years later, Spalding and family were at an Avis Rent A Car office. An omelet he'd eaten that morning was about to transform itself into gas. He wrote: "I was passing some of those ripe, slow, silent, hot burners, which I had no intention of taking responsibility for. I was easing them out so no one would hear them, while I stood there in the Avis office filling out rental car papers. But Forrest was standing next to me at nose level, and he, at the first whiff, cried out, 'Dad just farted!' "

That, by the way, is how one notices one has children.

Spalding the storyteller. People constitute a narrative species. We like to tell one another we're a *rational* species, but that's kind of a generally accepted joke. But a narrative species lives by stories, which is what we do. And, in this process, we silently elect a few to be the chief tellers of our tales. Thus Spalding.

The specialty of his storytelling was the search for a sorrow that could be alchemized into a myth—one that made you laugh. He went for the misery sufficiently deep to create a story we remembered.

So doing, he invented a form—a very rare thing among artists. Some called it the "epic monologue" because it was spoken and then it was written, like an epic, and it consisted of great and important themes drawn from the hero's life. But as an epic hero, Spalding stood on his head. Instead of having a single tragic flaw, he was *all* flaws—Spalding would have said that he crawled around on all flaws. And the one truly heroic element of his makeup was the willingness to be open—rabidly open—about his frailties.

At the same time, he knew that openness was his protection. The monologue kept him safe from others, just as did the table at which he sat, his set. The monologue protected him from dialogue.

No one was ever better at digressing from the story. Maybe Holden Caulfield, a kindred threatened nomadic spirit. Remember when Holden was in speech class, and the other students were coached to cry out "Digression! Digression!" whenever a speaker wandered from the straight and narrow of the subject. Spalding composed a *life* of digressions. For him, "Where was I?" was never a rhetorical question.

Missed opportunities, missed appointments, missed dates—all confessed in that unmistakable voice of unbuttered toast, frequently in this theater, where we honor him. He said: "I'm interested in creative confession. I would have made a great Catholic." Not to be parochial, but I think he would have made a better Jew. I think he *did* make a better Jew—free to be guilty as hell without the safety net of ritual. Specifically, he'd have made a great Oscar Levant, deliciously in control of his chaos, for as long as he could be. Turning the noise in his head into music.

And so oddly funny.

Once he rattled himself by realizing that he had actually enjoyed a day. And then this: "After all," he wrote, "think of all that could have gone *wrong*."

Once he says that, of course, he's off to Spalding Land, and we know we're in for a monstrous inventory of all that could have gone wrong that day: corrosive diseases; attacks from outer space; financial ruin; Kathie coming down with chronic fatigue syndrome, forcing him to take care of the household—until we feel, as he intended, that it was a *disastrous* day, not a good one. And, instead of being content, we are hurled into an imagined depression. No one ever could be so sublimely miserable.

That was a key to Spalding, I think. He could dream into what he knew. He could imagine what had already happened. And so, by looking back, he could rescue the rest of us. He survived like a champ. He kept his head above water—which is why, today, the cover of *Swimming to Cambodia* with Spalding's face half-submerged breaks our hearts.

His last adventure, perhaps next to last, occurred on a ferryboat that travels between two islands. He had something unknown on his mind. There was that ferryboat in mythology that traveled between the realms of the living and the dead. There was that quotation he liked from Eliot's *Four Quartets*, about one forever exploring, and then arriving where one started out, and seeing it for the first time. Life as exploration, and life as a trap. Back and forth. His famous dilemma from *The Killing Fields*: "I didn't know whether to become a social worker for the Cambodians, or get a Hollywood agent."

Exploration and trap. Back and forth.

He remarked of his mother's suicide that occurred when he was a child that it seemed like Brueghel's *Fall of Icarus*. He might have been speaking of his own death. Icarus, too, in the painting, descended into water, unnoticed by everyone—except, of course, by Brueghel. And by Spalding. Spalding noticed *everything*.

In the end, he discovered the misery sufficiently deep to create a story we remember. The story is Spalding, and it is of the mind so exquisitely attuned to itself that it made of itself a work of art.

One will remember the life. One will remember the posture and the look—supremely confident in its insecurity. Cute, playful, baffled. And one will remember the very good guy who, in spite of his torments, or because of them, struggled to enlighten our lives. To give them light. He does that still.

Mark Russell is an independent producer/curator of live performance events, most recently producing the Under the Radar festival. For twenty-one years he was the Artistic-Executive Director of Performance Space 122. *Life Interrupted* was one of the last productions he personally oversaw at P.S. 122.

Mark Russell

A table, a glass of water, a spiral notebook, and a mic.

I first saw Spalding Gray on the cover of the paperback version of Sam Shepard's *Tooth of Crime.* He was Hoss, shaved head, beard, body twisting away from Crow. I was an undergrad at the University of Texas searching for some theater equivalent to rock and roll. It looked like Spalding Gray.

Turn the journal pages forward a few years and I'm in New York watching Spalding in *Rumstick Road*—chasing Libby Howes and Ron Vawter around the tiny set. Chasing the dark nightmare of his mother's suicide. A true story—a true thing.

And so began Spalding's journey of discovery. He broke it down after all the wild chaos and frenzy of *Three Places in Rhode Island* to a table, a glass of water, a spiral notebook, and a mic. Poor theater, a man and an audience and a story.

Spalding sitting at that table, speaking into the mic, calling forth the script of his life from his memory and those notebooks. A simple ritual, part news report, part confessional, part American raconteur. *Sex and Death to the Age 14*. One man piecing his life back together, one memory, one true thing at a time.

Like all genius things it was a simple idea turned on its axis to become absolutely fresh and radical.

I loved to see Spalding's shows early in their development—to catch him in the act of discovering his own story. As the performances progressed, the show would build up steam through repetition and editing to become the snappy, racing tall tales he spun for the big paying customers uptown.

The theater that Spalding invented opened the door for hundreds of artists to make live events out of their own experience; it gave permission for the theater of Tim Miller and Holly Hughes, Lisa Kron, and so many others. It was a theater of identity—personal politics—a way to unearth stories that had not been told.

Now we take the solo performance form as a fact, but Spalding broke the door down. He was the original. The master. Sliding down his own slippery slope of a life, taking us with him.

In the late nineties, Spalding came to work at P.S. 122, making his last two pieces on Monday and Sunday nights, where our audience got to watch him build his performances one memory at a time. One perfect moment on top of another.

I found an old school desk on Houston Street, bought it, stripped it of gum and old paint, and stained it myself in the play yard of P.S. 122, so he would have a special table to work on when he visited. We kept a cold beer backstage for him post-show, Anchor Steam Liberty Ale. The tech crew made provisions to iron his plaid shirt each week, not ordinarily used to costume duty.

When he was making *Morning, Noon and Night* we would go out to the Telephone Bar afterward. I'd watch as he and Kathie walked home to Wooster Street down Second Avenue like young lovers. He seemed like one of the happiest men in the world.

Morning, Noon and Night became one of his most beloved pieces. Spalding actually grows up and finds a family. Miraculous. Somehow it gave me strength to start my own family.

Karen Finley took his table and upended it as the set for her *Honey* piece.

Then came the Black Spot. The accident in Ireland that aged him twenty years in a split second. Of course there would be a piece about it; it was rich with premonitions, heroism, absurd comedy.

We were planning a long string of workshop performances, which we had to cancel when Spalding chose to attempt to jump off a bridge two weeks before performances were to begin. He was talked down from that ledge. This was going to be a longer, harder story.

Paul Zaloom and I visited him in the hospital, a lockdown ward straight out of Kesey's *Cuckoo's Nest.* Spalding just lay there in the dark answering in monosyllables.

"Are you writing, Spalding?"

"No."

"Do you look out the window?"

"No."

Thank god for Paul and his ability to keep up a patter. It was scary to see someone as physical and engaged as Spalding at such a low point. I could barely say a word to him.

A few months later my son was born just a few floors below in the same hospital wing.

In the spring of 2003 we decided to try again. The show had a new title: *Life Interrupted.*

We had to cancel the first weekend of performances due to some more physical complications. I remember waiting with the tech crew for the second weekend. Would he show up? He did—just a few minutes before curtain—and began again. The table, the tall glass of water, the spiral notebook, and the mic. We skipped the beer backstage—traded for hot tea this time.

The first few shows barely clocked in at

thirty-five minutes. I got a couple of letters from disgruntled patrons expecting the happy, witty Spalding, but we didn't have to refund any tickets.

Then slowly the old Spalding Gray started coming back. He came alive behind that table. He found more humor and rhythm each week in the material. The piece grew in length and complexity. He was gaining energy, becoming more animated onstage and off. I felt he was healing himself through the act of performing. We were all witnesses to this act of recovery, participants in reclaiming a life.

Part of the work was a story Spalding read that starred him and his son Theo. Theo took to jumping up from his seat in the audience and taking bows with his dad at the later performances. There were standing ovations.

We ended the run on December 15. It was

the last public performance for Spalding. He left the table, glass of water, and mic, took the notebook, and headed home with Kathie.

We were making plans for a return workshop in April—this time to take the story through the great national interruption, 9/11.

I needed Spalding to walk me through that one. I was counting on him to tell his part of the story, make sense of it, find truth in it, and help me, and the P.S. 122 audience, reconnect with the journeys we started before that day— to reach through the craziness and grief to find the perfect moment—a true thing.

We won't get that part of the story. All P.S. 122 has left is the table, the glass, and the mic. Waiting for him to swim back to the surface and continue to tell us the rest of the journey. One wishes for closure, and then you get it. Like a black spot, a life interrupted. A long, wonderful monologue, cut short.

Robert Stein is a child psychoanalyst and family/adult therapist associated with the Tavistock Clinic in London. Presently, he lives and works in Sag Harbor and Manhattan. He also writes about a wide range of topics, from contemporary art to sleep, as well as mindfulness as a model for understanding children. He is one of Theo's godparents.

Robert Stein

I have been thinking about what I would like to say in memory of Spalding. He pretty much said it all. But these are public references, monologues, films, and memoirs. And while within this work he spoke of relationships with irony and candor, this work is only a partial picture of his legacy. I would like to take a moment to remember Spalding not as a performer, but as a father.

He had a profound love for Marissa, Forrest, and Theo. His relationship to them enriched his life immeasurably. I find it especially important to think of this today, if for no other reason than to affirm what has been overshadowed by the tragedy of his death.

If you spent time around Spalding when he was with the kids, it was quickly apparent that he didn't censor himself. He was not the kind of dad who backed off of difficult questions or emotional moments. Spalding said what he thought when it came to talking with his children. Sometimes he talked about outrageous things. He was never sure he had the right answer to simple questions, but he was willing to speculate and that was a good thing, for he often claimed to be a literal thinker, incapable of being truly imaginative.

Fatherhood shifted this for him. His children taught him to be playful with ideas.

In *Morning, Noon and Night* you get a glimpse of the relationship he had to these kids. But it is just a glimpse. Spalding as a father intensely listened to his children, his attention was holding—in the way that arms hold the body, his focus held their minds.

But he was not only a cerebral father. When he was well he danced joyously and beamed being in a room with kids careening around him and music blaring.

He really was in touch with his children when he was in touch with himself, and in my way of thinking he was seamlessly in touch with himself when he was with his children. He was present as a father. This dimension surprised even him. In better days he and I would take walks, and we'd talk about all manner of things, including his thoughts about Marissa and the boys.

He was impressed with Marissa's intelligence. He believed she understood his depth. His reflections about her were sincere and loving.

Spalding felt a connection with Forrest that he often said transcended any experience he had ever had. They met walking when he was an infant and walked the earth together. Spalding rediscovered the world walking and talking to Forrest. He loved Forrest's intuitive intelligence, his quiet way of learning, his perseverance, his passion for music, his passionate nature as a whole.

He loved the gifts of his gifted sons.

Theo's gift was another matter altogether—in a way he's Spalding unleashed. Theo knew how to play, he knew how to dance, and he was a mime and a clown—just about from birth. For a man who said he never laughed, Theo made him laugh. Theo climbed on his dad like a monkey in the wild, and Spalding loved it. He found joy in the way Theo played in the world, fearless, trusting, and full of energy.

This was my experience with Spalding as a father. He was loving, intellectual, and inquisitive about the way his children developed. He was relentless in his wish to be truthful. He was affectionate and physically strong. He loved telling family stories and didn't hesitate to share what was on his mind. His children taught him to play and showed him a wonderful world outside himself, which in itself was no easy task. What Spalding defeated in becoming a dad was his own need to be the child. He grew up, and I liked that about him.

It's hard to remember this man sometimes— in light of the damaged man who returned from Ireland—the old dad, as Forrest called him.

But I do. Every day something new pops up. Slowly he's coming back to life, into focus. I only wish that my experience of this passage of memory takes hold for his family as well.

Thank you.

Eric Stoltz is an actor and director who has appeared on Broadway, off Broadway, film, and television.

Eric Stoltz

I knew Spalding for a brief yet intense period of time in the late 1980s. We did the play *Our Town* together on Broadway, and since it was a huge cast we shared a dressing room about the size of this podium. For about half a year we shared this space.

During that time he was working on his latest monologue, writing a book or something, always engaged in some sort of creative pursuit outside the play—but mostly he would sit and think. With the lights out. He would spend a great deal of time just thinking in our room.

I remember just about every night—we both had a curious habit of showing up at the theater far too early—every night I'd come into our dressing room to find the lights out and candles lit; he was either napping on a mat or meditating in some yoga pose. I'd convince him to turn on the lights only to find our minuscule shared desk piled high with books, manuscript, and the occasional underground film.

I'd ask where they came from, and the answer was almost always, "Some guy stopped me on the subway and gave me this" or "I've got two tickets from a stranger for this pan-pipe concert in the East Village, wanna go? Renée hates this stuff."

"Spud," as we called him, was a true collector and seemed wide open to whatever anyone would give him. People would approach him, steer him off in a direction that hadn't occurred to him, and he'd try it. He was totally available in a way that most people (let alone famous people) aren't . . . he refused to elevate himself and be driven. He loved his walking—after the show, all the way from Times Square down to his loft in SoHo, navigating the city as though he was on a nature hike. Often I'd walk partway home with him, and it was no surprise to find that he was constantly being collared by strangers and street people, bumping into someone who was a friend of someone he sort of knew, getting into conversations with everyone and anyone . . . and he seemed to truly enjoy it. He wasn't jaded or even suspicious—he was always a tad dubious, but he'd talk himself out of it. It was wonderful to know someone in this city with a lack of boundaries who seemed to seek out encounters with the very people that most of us avoid almost intuitively. He was not the archetypical laid-back, repressed New Englander that he played so often in movies— he was driven and energetically curious and highly charged.

He was even quite passionate in his darker moments. I recall his seemingly unnatural hatred of Dean & Deluca—he truly despised them. I can't remember the exact details, but as a result I've never gone into one of their stores since. And he wasn't too fond of theater critics, either. (At this point, I would urge all of you to avoid Dean & Deluca, and theater critics, in memory of Spalding.)

To me he was like an odd, questing hero, always searching for that perfect accidental moment or divine happening. He once described himself as a cross between Huck Finn and Candide. Naturally—and some found this surprising, back then before he had a family of his own—he loved the children in our show. Their relentless teasing and energy and inability to suppress anything always made him laugh.

His favorite moment in our play, I think, wasn't even in the script—it was when Shane

Culkin, playing eleven-year-old Wally Webb, threw up onstage during a performance. Twice. Projectile vomited. It was an amazing moment, and Spalding spoke of it with perverse glee and awe for months to come, eventually even putting it into one of his monologues.

He was single-minded in his pursuit of something pure and true—it really did seem like a quest. When it came to his appearance, however, it seemed he couldn't be bothered, always wearing the same wide-wale cords and flannelly kind of shirt. He even had to be reminded when to cut his hair. It was as though all the things that we're inundated with in our society, all the things we're told are vital and important and meaningful—fame, money, image—were afterthoughts (if even that) to him. Although he would confess on occasion that he wouldn't mind having great amounts of any of them, it wasn't as though he pursued them. As I recall, he didn't have a publicist and didn't understand why anyone would.

He loved doing *Our Town*—he called it a great spiritual and deeply existential play, and he spoke of how it became a kind of meditation for him, saying the words eight times a week.

It was the third act, I think, that resonated with him. That act deals with eternity and what matters in life. I always felt that those questions and thoughts were very close to Spalding, that it spoke to him, and consequently to us through him. And it's those ideas that come to mind and stay with me when I think of him now—the bigger, more meaningful, intangible thoughts and ideas that seemed to me to fuel his quest.

He will be much missed.

OLD WHALER'S CHURCH
SAG HARBOR

May 15, 2004

George Coates was the theater director and producer responsible for introducing Spalding Gray to San Francisco audiences in 1980 when he was Artistic Director of the San Francisco International Theatre Festival. He presented Spalding Gray's early monologues, including *Sex and Death to the Age 14, India (and After)*, and *A Personal History of the American Theater* at the Intersection Theater. In 1982 he invited Spalding to return to San Francisco to perform *Interviewing the Audience*, a series of one-on-one encounters with individuals selected from the audience. George Coates's stage works have appeared at numerous theater festivals in Japan and Europe and in the United States at the Brooklyn Academy of Music's BAM Festival and the Kennedy Center Opera House.

George Coates

The evening that Spalding chose to go over the rail was the coldest night in New York Harbor in decades. The following day all the ferryboats to Staten Island would be frozen in. But on this night the freezing winds were so intense that access to the outer deck of the ferry was forbidden. Spalding asked one of the passengers why there was suddenly a rope barrier blocking access to the outer deck that hadn't been there before.

Spalding claimed that he never made things up. Not true. He embellished, he exaggerated, and he left a lot of things out. He once told me (and this might not have happened because he said it was true) that he came to believe he could make a living as a storyteller after realizing how much time and money he had spent waiting for his therapist to stop laughing.

Everyone knows that Spalding wrote in English, but few people are aware that he meditated in three languages. He was fluent in the languages of Chance, Fate, and Necessity. He knew how to read their signs, which led him to conclude that "things do not happen for a reason. They just happen." On the surface it was a liberating insight, but the thought was disturbing to him in its implication that perhaps this moment is all there is, with no immortal afterlife or sequel to follow. Life is now, and if not, we are limited in our capacity to know otherwise.

And so, being the good pantheist that he was, he drew strength from the world around him, paying careful attention to the ordinary miracles of chance events, and ever mindful of the fate that awaits, he confronted his fears by indulging in them to the point of hypochondriacal exhaustion. I would ask him, "Spalding, why do you keep placing yourself in situations that result in these endless cycles of regret and lament?" To which he would respond, "I am drawn to the study of extreme psychic states," which was his way of admitting to the fact that he found himself fascinating.

He was a fascinating study of extreme psychic states who mocked his demons by dancing with them morning, noon and night until he had some idea of their hidden meaning and could name them. Because names matter. Not so much because they were meaningful, but because they carried messages.

In *Life Interrupted*, Spalding says the driver of the van in the accident in Ireland was named Murphy. He remembers the nurse attending him was named Murphy. When he returned

home the realtor who sold the house he regret-
ted losing was named Murphy. He asked the
audience, "Am I caught in the grip of some cos-
mic Murphy's Law?"

Spalding's enormous capacity for self-exam-
ination is well known but not so well known
was the degree to which he demanded to be
abducted into other people's lives. He could be
struck dumb by a random display of natural
beauty. A grove of elm trees could render him
speechless. He believed that getting lost in a
familiar neighborhood was an undervalued
pleasure to share with close friends from out
of town.

For Spalding the personal was the political,
but not always at the same time. He was very
promiscuous in his generosity. He never said
no to the unending requests for benefit appear-
ances in support of nonprofit theaters, a free
Tibet, or to dismantle a nuclear power plant.

When he discussed his mother's suicide in his monologues he did it partly to inoculate himself against succumbing to a similar fate. Spalding used to say that one of the things that troubled him most about death was the fact that he would not be able to tell the story of his own personal encounter with it. But he did come very, very close.

On that fateful January night in New York Harbor on the Staten Island ferry, two strangers struck up a conversation with Spalding. According to a letter describing the encounter published in the *New York Times:* Hugo Perez, a writer, and his girlfriend Betsy were among the passengers boarding the ferry when Spalding overheard Betsy say, "Is that Spalding Gray?" Hugo, Betsy, and Spalding made awkward small talk and admired the Manhattan skyline. Then Spalding noticed that a rope cutting off access to the outer deck of the boat had appeared. "What's that rope doing there? It wasn't there before," he said. Hugo and Betsy didn't know the answer, but I am forever grateful that Hugo and Betsy were there with Spalding at that impossibly difficult moment.

Two strangers arriving from out of the audience to perform their assigned roles: Hugo Perez to tell the story leading up to Spalding's final moment, and Betsy, who has to be the most significant of significant others imaginable, given that Spalding's mother, Elizabeth, went by the name Betsy. Names matter.

Gracie Coates, daughter of George Coates and Colleen Larkin, has known Spalding Gray all her life. Spalding arrived at the hospital ten minutes after her birth on April 2, 1990, and he continued to be a friend until his disappearance. Gracie began writing "Rescue" when Spalding disappeared in January 2004 and completed it shortly after his body was discovered. She was then thirteen. She is currently in high school and continues to play piano and compose and sing her own songs. She lives in Berkeley, California.

Gracie Coates

Rescue

(A song written for Spalding Gray)

All these tears held deep inside of me
It's so painful and so hard to breathe
There's no way out anymore
Why can't it just be how it was before

His life like ice slowly melting away
He tried his best to be better every day
But sometimes you just can't hold on
    anymore
Why can't it just be how it was before

When I think about his beautiful life
I think about his three kids and his wife

And you'll be with us forever more
Why can't it just be how it was before

(PIANO BREAK)

Though your end here was like a torn
   collage
When I see you it's like this real mirage
And sometimes I feel you're right here
   next to me
Your decision has truly set you free

It's a rescue, it's a rescue I see
It's a rescue, it's a rescue by sea

William Farley grew up in Massachusetts. He now resides in San Francisco and has been making fiction and nonfiction films for more than thirty years.

William Farley

Words can illuminate our path
if we dare share our deepest fears
and forge a dialogue with the past.

Spalding Gray took many journeys
and we were blessed
to hitchhike
along.

Regardless of the terrain
he chose to cross
we were always grateful
for the glimpses of a landscape
we might have chosen to hide from
if we had our way.

Celebrating the Life of Spalding Gray

Armed with a sense of humor
that was larger
than our fears
he made us feel brave.

What more could be asked of Spalding
   Gray,
a man who dared craft words
that gently brought us
to visit
the unexamined assumptions of our day.

Rockwell Gray is Spalding's older brother. He teaches English at Washington University in St. Louis.

Rockwell Gray

Spalding, My Brother

When I realized my brother Spalding was unavailable to me, missing, and then dead, I knew that, aside from my wife, my closest partner through life was gone. With both our parents dead some years back, it was he alone who had shared with me the memory of that long stretch of years since we had been kids together in our "our town" of Barrington, Rhode Island. My younger brother Channing knew that world too, but he was nine years my junior and experienced our family in a different way from Spalding and me.

Barrington was a safe and beautiful place to grow up, along the edge of Narragansett Bay, and Spalding and I carried into our adult years a shared sense of what was right and wrong about it. Wrong, we agreed, were its bourgeois Republican complacency and its uptight WASP ways. Right were the lovely shelter it gave us and the feeling of the nearby ocean. Summers we spent together by the shore, riding the waves and making a hideout under our beach cottage. That was an extension of the early play we had had in our shared bedroom on Rumstick Road, where we created imagined worlds under the covers of our beds. I protected my little brother and hugged him down under those sheets, and my protection later extended to the schoolyard and the neighborhood.

Spalding always said that the arrival of baby Channing in 1947 turned my attention away from him, but in fact we remained close until I was expelled from public school and sent off to finish my sophomore year at Fryeburg Academy in Maine. I returned to find that my brother "Spud" had formed a circle of friends who were, like him, less interested in academic effort than I had become. While I was wrestling with Shakespeare and listening to classical music, he affected a Beat style, listened to jazz, and later purchased a motorcycle. But we still talked, and he still told at table the long, winding stories that had earned him his family reputation as a great fabricator who loved to dramatize the ordinary. His visit at a Catholic friend's church, for example, resulted in a wild tale about voodoo being performed by a man in a cape who mumbled strange formulas over a chalice and then passed it around to the kneeling parishioners.

When I went to college at nearby Brown University, Spalding too was sent to Fryeburg for his last two years of high school, but we wrote and remained close even then, and on our times at home together he would ply me with questions like "What is existentialism?" When he enrolled in theater arts at Emerson College in Boston, we were clearly on different tracks. I saw him choosing the more adventurous path.

Oddly, during those years the one thing we didn't talk of was our mother's periodic breakdowns, when she would seek out the help of Christian Science practitioners and even rest homes. Though she and I shared a sense of devotion to the church during my "reformed" teen years, I was gone for several years after college, and it was Spalding and Channing who lived through the worst of times at home, and Spalding who heard her speak of having a vision of Christ come to heal her. He it was who "dated" her when my father didn't want to go out and who kept her company on summer days by the water.

When Spalding began to perform in summer stock, I supported his choice of theater as a vocation when no one else in the family took it very seriously. For them, he was in a phase that probably would pass. But, to his annoyance, I brought pen and paper to the show, determined to give him a critique. What he really wanted of me, I soon realized, was unstinting approval and support. This I gave him when, some years later, he and Liz LeCompte and others did *Rumstick Road* at the Performing Garage in New York's SoHo. Spalding's decision to use tapes of family members speaking about my mother's final crisis and suicide was not well received at home, but I supported his choice. That piece and the larger work, *Three Places in Rhode Island*, was the start of his great autobiographical impulse that played itself out in the long string of monologues that followed.

For a time, I confess, I didn't understand the

basis of his success. I was skeptical of the growing acclaim. But in time I came to admire his
great gift for turning his daily experience into
art, and for making the theater his own mode
of therapy. It was always, of course, more than
that because it *was* artful and risky and funny
and desperate all at once. In the brilliant work
Swimming to Cambodia and the later monologues,
he left his mark on the history of the American
theater.

In his search for "the perfect moment,"
Spalding could be unrelentingly restless, unable
to stay with the ordinary moments that offered
themselves to him. Many a walk we shared on
which he worried to death the subject of such
fulfillment. But meanwhile we had many good
moments together. My wife and I trekked after
him to performance venues, and I received calls
from all corners of the country in which he reported his latest successes and his fear that

maybe the inspiration would run out. For all the marvelous success he had in later years, however, material goods and money meant relatively little to him. What did come to matter a great deal in the later years was his family with Kathie, Marissa, Forrest, and Theo. I took real pleasure in seeing him as a father, in knowing that he had reached that place that both Channing and I had earlier found for ourselves.

Since our mother's death in 1967 had left our original family without the maternal center that so often draws children back at holidays, the three of us generally did not gather for those occasions. One notable exception was this past Christmas (2003), which my wife and daughter and I shared with Kathie and Spalding and the kids in Sag Harbor. But Channing and his family were unable to be there, and Spalding himself was all but absent, deep in the throes of his private suffering.

We did not suppose he was then as near the end as he turned out to be, but his long silences before the crackling log fire should have raised my suspicions, for I recall his once musing that the worst thing about death was that one would be forced to stop talking, and as I remember him now, it is that voice, ceaselessly wondering and inventing and lamenting, that I missed then and so much miss now. It was the voice of the compulsive storyteller, and the voice at the other end of the phone line charged with excitement and simultaneous doubt about his next venture.

As I say that, I realize that the Spalding I loved—and love still—was the entire person who, whole or broken, kept trying to weave a web of meaning for his life. And he was the person who walked the Appalachian Trail with me, who made a mean pot of pea soup when I came to New York to visit, who took me sailing in his beetle boat out of Sag Harbor. The darkness of his last couple of years notwithstanding, he lived his life more fully than many of us manage to do. I am grateful today for that legacy he left all of us who loved him.

Let me close with a few words of Ralph Waldo Emerson, a distant cousin on my father's side: "Nothing is ever wholly lost. That which is excellent remains forever a part of the universe."

Larry Josephson has been a public radio personality for forty years, starting in the 1960s on WBAI in New York, were he was the enfant terrible of morning radio. He's now heard on NPR stations, including WNYC. He won a Peabody Award and three Grammy nominations for producing Bob and Ray CDs.

Larry Josephson

Over the twenty-five years I knew Spalding, he gave me great pleasure and many gifts. The gift of friendship, the pleasure of watching him work and grow as an artist, and one final magnificent gift.

The first gift is the monologues, Spalding's work. He taught me that you don't have to be Jewish to be neurotic, obsessed, and conflicted. When I first saw *Sex and Death to the Age 14*, I realized that Spalding, a New England WASP, and I, an L.A. Jew, had remarkably similar childhoods. The same anxieties about girls, parents, and peers—singular experience made universal through art. A lot of us call ourselves artists; Spalding really was—and what an artist.

The second gift was the gift of friendship. For a time, his shrink's office was near my house. After a session we would walk in Central Park. I told him my troubles, he listened attentively. He told me of his adventures on the road, in a low, confidential voice—*Don't breathe a word of this to anyone.* I thought I was his confessor, keeper of his secrets. Of course, the confidences he shared found their way into the next monologue.

The third gift was an introduction to new ideas and experiences. (I try never to leave my house.) Like "the other," "perfect moments," bits and pieces of Oriental philosophy and practice (Zen, yoga), vicarious travel to exotic places I would never get to, drugs I was afraid to take, and a sex life I could only envy. There was one pleasure I did permit myself, the pleasure of his ironic, subtle wit. Spalding didn't really get jokes—"A lobster and a horse walk into a bar, and the bartender says . . ."—that kind. (See me afterward for the rest of the joke.) But he made delicious fun of New Age gurus, radicals, hippies, the drug culture, and most of all, himself.

Spalding's last and greatest gift to me was given in the hospital. For this story to make sense I must tell you just a bit about my upbringing. I came of age in the '50s, the Eisenhower era. A time of prosperity, conformity, and emotional repression. *Ozzie and Harriet* was not too far from middle class reality. In my family, men did not hug each other, even in moments of grief. Showing feelings other than anger would be a sign of weakness. To kiss another man, was *just not done.* Even today, post-'60s, post–New Age, I'm still uncomfortable with displays of emotion, one on one. When my father died, I never cried—I just got depressed. Fast-forward to New York Hospital, the last time I saw Spalding. I was shocked—

the old Spalding was gone. Try as I might, I could not penetrate the brick wall of his depression and obsession. At the end of each visit I hugged him for dear life—and kissed him. My love for this man brought it out, spontaneously breached *my* wall. For this, I will always be grateful.

It is often said at memorials that Spalding is now at peace, his demons slain. I don't think so. Somewhere out there in the cosmos, Spalding is sitting at a little table, with a spiral notebook, a glass of water, and a microphone, doing a monologue for Lord Buddha or Jesus Christ or space aliens, trying to unravel the last day of his life on the ferry. "Should I, or shouldn't I," arguments with his mother, his family, and himself.

I'm sure the monologues will go on forever—in our memories and on the tapes and in the movies and the books he left behind. Spalding will always be talking to us.

Aviva Kempner is a writer and filmmaker who water-walks daily.

Aviva Kempner

One of the great pleasures of regularly attending opening night at the New York Film Festival was meeting Spalding. He could not have been more gracious and warm in responding to one of his fans and returned the favor by inquiring about my filmmaking.

I considered myself even luckier when shortly thereafter we coincidentally shared a train ride down to my Washington, D.C., home. And what a glorious train ride that was. The conversation flowed as fast as the train zoomed along the tracks.

Spalding—the most neurotic WASP I ever had the pleasure of knowing, a Wasp Jew—was the most entertaining friend I had. No conversation was without great storytelling and wit. He loved telling the story of arriving on the set with Sharon Stone and her declaring, "Another intellectual has arrived."

He also brought his wonderful wife, Kathie, and the kids into my life during numerous trips, either his visits to D.C. or mine to the Hamptons and Martha's Vineyard. I want you to know during one of his solo visits to D.C., when he and I had dinner together, the conversation always turned to his kids and how much he cared for them.

He taught me that Jews did not have a monopoly on questioning and self-doubts.

When I joked that in my next life I would have thin thighs and learn to ski, Spalding went about learning to ski at middle age—and creating a whole marvelous show about my greatest fear.

No, Spalding, I will never learn to ski in this

lifetime. But I never got to tell you that I did get over one fear you teased me about on Martha's Vineyard when you asked me in disbelief why I was there and not going swimming. I accepted your challenge and go to the pool almost daily—I just go water-walking in a pool and not to the ocean—but your teasing, Spalding, helped me to conquer one of my biggest hang-ups.

I know that Spalding was not able to conquer all his ghosts. Yet his talents and accomplishments should be inspirational to us all to live life to its fullest and take from life's richness in making our art.

No wonder his beloved wife and children became the subjects of his art. Seeing them we can behold his *best work.*

Marissa Maier is a sophomore at Sarah Lawrence College, where she's concentrating in the writer's program.

Marissa Maier

During my senior year at the Ross School in East Hampton, I wrote an essay on the impact a depressed person has on their family and friends. A majority of my essay focused on my own personal experience of living with someone who was extremely depressed. The following is an excerpt from my essay:

> *Living with my stepfather, after his accident, was one of the most difficult phases of my life. As time progressed he sank further and further into the deepest depression imaginable; and nothing seemed to ease his pain. He spent all day either in bed or ruminating in his armchair in the living room.*

In that armchair, he spent hours thinking about all the things the accident had taken away from him. The accident had fractured his head and had taken away his handsome face. The accident had left him with a drop foot and had taken away his ability to be the active person he used to be. The accident had caused brain damage and thus had taken away his ability to create moving, yet funny, monologues, the thing that he had built his career, and subsequently his life, around.

Yet all of these things paled in comparison to what had really been taken away, his ability to love and to live. After the accident, he lost the ability to experience joy, to convey love, to laugh, and to feel anything except the bitter mental pain that followed him everywhere he went.

His inability to live, however, was relatively tolerable compared to his numerous suicide attempts. Living with him during this time was like

237

walking on eggshells; at any time he could slip out of the house and go to the town bridge, where he repeatedly tried to kill himself.

After each attempt the notion of him recovering to his old self became more and more futile. Following each attempt, I would lie in bed wondering if my family would be better without him. As time wore on, however, I knew that the answer to that question was without a doubt yes.

That is why, when the day came that he succeeded in killing himself, I wasn't angry with him. He was living in excruciating mental pain that I don't think any of us could have comprehended. When he killed himself the prevailing emotion I had was sadness. I mourned the fact that I would never hear another one of his bitingly funny jokes or never see another one of his moving performances again.

I can imagine him doing it. I can imagine him struggling to get over the railing, trying desperately to get his old and injured limbs over the metal barrier. I can imagine him standing there for just a moment as he grasped onto the railing, and then he let go, he finally let go of all of it, all the weight that had burdened his spirit and his heart for the past two and a half years. I think that in that moment he was finally free.

M. J. Bruder Munafo is the Artistic Director of the Vineyard Playhouse on Martha's Vineyard, Massachusetts.

M. J. Bruder Munafo

The Great Adventure of Spalding Gray

There is an antique oak table in our house that we call "Spalding's table." A nice table, really. Simple. Once upon a time, Spalding Gray came to the Island to perform *Gray's Anatomy* at the Vineyard Playhouse. The tech requirements for the main set piece, a table, were extremely specific. I was producing his show and so I invited him over to inspect this particular table. As things turned out, it was perfect. So, several times over the next ten years, my husband Paul and I would clear it off, give it a polish, and turn it over to Spalding. This table is

Reprinted with permission from the *Vineyard Gazette*.

strong enough to hold many tales, and it is heavy. I write these recollections on it now. Perhaps its memory is better than mine.

I knew Spalding Gray: the great American monologuist, the loving dad, the careful observer of the world around him. I knew him through some of his happiest moments and then the darkest. What began as a professional relationship almost instantly became a friendship. At the theater I am privileged to meet and work with many talented and interesting people. Once in a while, if you can keep your head above the intensity and illusion of the theater world, you are lucky to get to know a little of the real person.

Spalding was crazy about the Vineyard, and he arrived that first year in high spirits. With him were Kathie, the new love of his life, and Forrest, his beautiful baby son. He seemed astonished but quite pleased at the turn of events in his recent life. Kathie is a beautiful woman, strong and fit, real smart and with a sense of humor. Their relationship was exciting and lasting. This was a new life for them, and Paul and I were new friends.

That first time and in the summers that followed, the Island worked its magic, as it always does, beginning with the ferry ride across Vineyard Sound. Sunburnt and wind-blown, Spalding would instantly relax into a summer routine of rising at dawn and celebrating spectacular sunsets from his favorite rented cottage overlooking Menemsha Harbor. He practically shouted with glee when he reached the ocean, "the sea" as he called it. He was a champion body surfer all the day long on the grand waves at Quansoo. He and Kathie loved to explore the Vineyard on way-too-long bike rides, first with Forrest and then Theo, strapped into a baby seat on back.

Like many prominent summer residents, they were invited to and attended illustrious up-Island dinners and cocktail parties on gleaming yachts in Edgartown Harbor. Paul and I used to tease him that we were relegated to live vicariously through his stories of these events. Marvelous, funny stories.

Spending time with Spalding or just conversing on the telephone could be a great adventure. It was hard not to hang on his every word because he was so sharp and awfully funny in his extraordinary observations of ordinary life. He was fascinated by other people and enjoyed spontaneous and unconventional encounters with strangers and fans alike. His fans came from all walks of life and were devoted.

He made many friends on the Vineyard and visited often with his oldest Island connection, the artist Rez Williams. Rez and I have been in regular touch since Spalding's disappearance, trying to piece things together as best we can. He told me that he first saw Spalding, many, many years ago, performing Samuel Beckett's *Krapp's Last Tape*. He played an old man sitting at a table with a tape recorder and a microphone. Pause.

A few times during the Island's off-season we got together with Spalding, Kathie, and the kids in New York.

He invited us to the gala Broadway opening of *Morning, Noon and Night* at Lincoln Center and I remember we were some of the last to leave the Penthouse reception afterward, helping Kathie to escort sleepy children away.

We went again to New York to see him on-stage in Gore Vidal's *The Best Man* and his performance was impressive. We congratulated him and he accepted but then complained about the rigors of playing in a Broadway show eight times a week. His character's name was Bill Russell. Coincidentally, at intermission, Paul and I had run into another Bill Russell, the painting contractor from Vineyard Haven who was there to see the play. So we introduced him to Spalding at the stage door afterward and all got a big kick out of it.

When Spalding performed at the Playhouse, we had a simple routine to follow: iron his flannel shirt and provide fresh spring water. He'd arrive at the theater after a massage—he loved massages—he'd complete a sound check on the stage, and then meditate and pace (if one can do both) in the dressing room while drinking tea until it was time for "places."

His shows were always sold out and audiences murmured with great expectation. His voice was mesmerizing and we were soon under his spell. He was the consummate storyteller.

After the show, he'd be anxious to hear how we thought it went. He liked to record his new works-in-progress so he could listen to himself and, more important, listen for the audiences' responses to the material. Spalding was extremely generous and supportive of live theater and the Playhouse. We had a mutual respect for each other. He often agreed to participate in benefit performances and joined our Honorary Board of Directors.

Once he came to the Island in November to record *It's a Slippery Slope* in James Taylor's studio. At supper one night, he talked about the quiet beauty of the Vineyard autumn and how he missed his family. He loved Kathie and his boys and his stepdaughter Marissa very much.

A few times over the years, we also produced his shows at other Island venues: the Old Whaling Church, Union Chapel, and the MV Regional High School's Performing Arts Center.

One night at the Old Whaling Church, a woman near the back fainted and an ambulance was called. Emergency lights flashed endlessly around the church for what seemed forever. Spalding never missed a beat and I think some audience members even thought the lights were part of the show. He was a true professional and in complete command of his craft.

Which is why it was so hard to see him struggling toward the end. After an auto accident in Ireland, he was never quite the same. This has been reported in detail in all the papers and there is no need to say more on the matter because it was true.

But the last time I saw him, I detected a glimmer of light in his eye and just a flicker of a smile—the old Spalding was back for a moment. And that is whom I will remember, and miss, for many summers. Long Pause.

Kathleen Russo is Spalding Gray's widow and the mother of Marissa, Forrest, and Theo. In 1997, she cofounded Washington Square Arts, an arts management company for a diverse group of performing artists located in New York City.

Kathleen Russo

*My relationship with Spalding started off tur-*bulent fourteen years ago and, unfortunately, ended turbulent four months ago. However, the middle stretch of our relationship was— and Spalding never allowed this word to be used in our home unless something like this happened—awesome.

When I first met Spalding at the Rochester Airport on Friday, January 13, 1990, I had a feeling my life was about to drastically change. Maybe it was the way he looked at me as we were looking for a desk for his performance. I looked at him sitting behind this antique desk and went into a trance. I couldn't put my finger on it, but I felt like I'd known Spalding already and he would become someone very important in my life.

The second time we got together in Toronto, I blurted out that we would have beautiful children together. This really scared him because he said no one had ever said that to him before.

I knew he would be an excellent father from the get-go, just by observing him play with my three-year-old daughter, Marissa, or watching him work with a group of inner-city kids at a residency on Block Island. What a great father he came to be! Although it came late in life, it came naturally and he embraced it with open arms and heart. All three children felt love, respect, and an honesty that they didn't encounter too often with other adults. He made each child feel special from the moment he entered their life—Marissa at three, Forrest at eight months, and Theo at birth. He gave the children the support and nurturing they needed for their foundation that will stay with them always. They received from him a wild wisdom that expanded their imagination and creativity.

Marissa loved the way he encouraged her to write and how he gave her the belief she could do it. Forrest loved his first drum set Spalding bought him at age five and how he cried the last time he watched Forrest play. Theo loved the way he danced with him and twirled him around to all kinds of music. He's dancing for his father here today.

I loved the way he made me laugh. Laughter was the glue in the relationship. It brought us together and bonded us, even in the darkest times. I loved the way he made me feel beautiful, special, and appreciated. I loved our compatibility and how we never held anything back from each other.

I loved the way Spalding would try anything with me (at least once)—from the Ice Hotel in

Canada, boogie boarding in Martha's Vineyard during a storm, paragliding with Forrest in Greece, all the sails on his boat small and how we'd crash into the rocks before we even got out of the harbor, hiking in Santa Cruz and worrying about the mountain lions attacking us, driving on the Hana Highway in a car full of children and me screaming for him to please drive five miles per hour, our first camping trip in the Adirondacks and worrying about the bears, and skiing first runs in Aspen at six A.M., to the simplicity of holding his child and singing at morning program at Sag Harbor Elementary.

I loved his generosity to the children, to me, to our friends and the world. He contributed so much in his sixty-two years of life. He left our family not with a life half lived but a life fully lived.

I look at our children and know I'll always have Spalding by my side—checking in and feeling the love and the pride I do each time I look into their eyes. For that, I say thank you, Spalding, for creating this family with me.

I know he felt this was the only way to end his pain. I respect and try to understand his decision. I promise him that he will always remain a major part of our family's daily lives.

The last time I saw Spalding was almost fourteen years to the day we first met. On the freezing cold morning of January 10, I helped him carry his skis and bags down the stairs to the car waiting outside to take him to the airport for a ski vacation—my Christmas present to him. At six in the morning, we stood outside our building, looked into each other's eyes, kissed and hugged each other, and he said, "Thanks for the trip, honey." I said, "You never call me honey. You must really be looking forward to this trip." And he was.

We'll miss him forever. Spalding, Spalding—my partner for life. Now you've gone somewhere else and left a big hole in my heart. I know time will help heal this aching and our children will resume full and rewarding lives in this wonderful community of Sag Harbor, a community we both were committed to raising our children in and a place we wanted to live the rest of our lives.

I love you, Spalding.

About the Author

Writer, actor, and performer Spalding Gray was the author of *It's a Slippery Slope, Swimming to Cambodia, Monster in a Box, Morning, Noon and Night,* and *Impossible Vacation,* among other works. He appeared on Broadway in his own one-man shows and in an acclaimed revival of *Our Town* and Gore Vidal's *The Best Man,* on PBS and HBO, and in numerous films, including Roland Joffe's *The Killing Fields,* David Byrne's *True Stories,* and more recently Steven Soderbergh's *Gray's Anatomy.* He was working on *Life Interrupted* at the time of his death in 2004.